American Woodys

THE CRESTLINE SERIES

American Woodys

DONALD F. WOOD

First published in 2001 by MBI Publishing Company, Galtier Plaza, Suite 200, 380 Jackson Street, St. Paul, MN 55101-3885 USA

MBI Publishing Company books are also available at discounts in bulk quantity for industrial or sales-promotional use. For details write to Special Sales Manager at Motorbooks International Wholesalers & Distributors, Galtier Plaza, Suite 200, 380 Jackson Street, St. Paul, MN 55101-3885 USA.

Library of Congress Cataloging-in-Publication Data Available
ISBN 0-7603-0866-7

Edited by Greg Field
Printed in the United States of America

On the front cover, upper left: This 1942 Mercury wagon belongs to William Ironside, of Michigan. It was originally sold to Edward Kingsford, a Ford-Mercury dealer in Iron Mountain, Michigan, who also happened to be married to a cousin of Henry Ford. Kingsford was also in the real estate business and supplied some of the timberlands that supplied the lumber used to build Ford and Mercury station wagon bodies. In addition, he had a charcoal plant that utilized wood scraps from the Ford wagon body-building plant. *Louis Ironside* **Upper right:** John Winter, of Arizona, owns this 1951 Dodge. It has a Cantrell body and has been completely restored. Winter installed a four-speed gearbox and a regular clutch to replace the wagon's original fluid drive, which made the wagon too sluggish to operate in today's traffic. *John Winter* **Lower left:** This restored 1923 Buick belongs to the Ironside family in Michigan. The body was built by Cantrell. It is constructed of white ash and has maple inserts. The spare tire appears to block the driver's door. *Louis Ironside* **Lower right:** The roofline of the 1947 Nash suburban sedan slopes downward in the rear, rather than having the boxy shape and extra room of a conventional station wagon body. *Betty and Jim Fritts*

On the back cover, top: William J. Franz, of Maryland, owns this 1950 DeSoto wagon. *William J. Franz* **Center:** Restoration of the Ames Packard took three years. The dark wood is mahogany; the light wood is ash. The body color is authentic Packard chicory green. *Mike Ames* **Bottom:** Betty and Jim Fritts, of Florida, own this 1942 Hudson Six station wagon, which they purchased in 1989. In the early 1990s, they had it completely restored to original factory condition. It's painted green. *Betty and Jim Fritts*

CONTENTS

DEDICATION

to Kayla

My granddaughter, Kayla, wears her Santa Cruz woody shirt as she stands next to various small woody items.

Preface

Wooden station wagons—"woodys"—belong to the first half of the twentieth century. Many survive because of their unique beauty and collector interest. After writing mostly about trucks, I am pleased to write a book about woodys because it allows me to discuss a vehicle type that shares passenger car, bus, and truck characteristics. Two other books I wrote for MBI may help establish my background for this topic: *Chevy El Camino, 1959-1982*, published in 1982, covered a vehicle that clearly shared auto and truck features and was purchased by individuals who wanted some of both. *American Buses*, published in 1998, dealt with vehicles, usually larger than autos, that carried primarily passengers. I've written other books focused on trucks in various vocational applications requiring specialized bodies. For the first half of the century, many truck bodies were built partially, or completely, of wood. Some of the shops noted for their station wagon bodies had an equally fine reputation for their truck bodies.

On early station wagons, wood was used to construct the frame, and panels were used between the frame pieces. Later, metal was used for the framing, and wood served in only a decorative role, much as one might put wooden paneling in a recreation room. In the 1950s, the use of real wood in station wagon bodies ceased.

Definitions used by old car and truck collectors are not "watertight." They are "umbrellas" under which many different models can fit. Also, some vehicles can fit under more than one collector umbrella. While most woody station wagons are thought of as having an auto's front end and a squarish wooden body, a few post–World War II convertible coupes and sedans were built with attractive wooden trim, and today these

vehicles are welcome at any woody meet. In addition, many vehicles with homemade wooden bodies were built and often used as campers. They are included in this book as reminders of how frequently wood was used for building small vehicle bodies; one can see many examples that some of today's readers could match in their home workshops.

Many woody enthusiasts are equally interested in wood-bodied trucks. The line between station wagons and trucks is hard to draw. Often they shared nearly the same body, with the possible difference being interior seating or the size or placement of rear windows. Some body builders used almost the same body for their station wagons as for their panel or open-sided peddler's trucks. For those reasons, the book contains some pictures of wooden truck bodies. Wood was widely used in truck bodies and its decline and disappearance occurred for reasons similar to those causing its decline in usage for station wagons.

Many of the photos come from my collection; others were kindly supplied by owners of individual station wagons. There already exist other books on station wagons, and owners' groups publish very informative newsletters. The very active National Woody Club has many meets that attract wagons; I attended two: one on the pier at Santa Cruz, California, and the other at Wavecrest (just north of San Diego, California). Some of the pictures selected for this book were chosen because they showed pictures of makes of bodies or chassis with bodies that have not appeared elsewhere.

Unlike old-truck and fire-apparatus collectors, who are nearly all male, many woody owners appear to be husband-and-wife teams. There may be two explanations for this: One would be that station wagons are a type of vehicle style with which women can easily identify. A second reason would be that the amount of money needed to buy and/or restore a "woody" is so great that any husband would have to sweet-talk his wife to get her involved and committed to the vehicle purchase and restoration process.

Many people who restore old station wagons appear to be wealthy and refined, possibly trying to emulate the social circles that owned and operated woodys a half century ago. However, station wagons also had an earthier side. Patrick Ertel, editor of *This Old Truck*, wrote the following in the January 2000/2001 issue in response to a reader who preferred that Ertel devote less space to station wagon topics:

> Station wagons are kind of a gray area in more ways than one. Old wagons, depot hacks, suburbans, and so on, seem to be regarded differently than newer station wagons. People also think of wagons differently based on their differing experiences with them. Many were used as family haulers, and those who remember them that way don't consider them commercial vehicles. My grandfather operated a painting business. He always bought old station wagons because they were cheap, and after he was finished with one, it was totally unusable. When I think of a station wagon, I think with fondness of a beat-up work vehicle with ladders strapped to the roof and various colors of house paint all over it.

A number of individuals, organizations, and firms assisted with this book, and they include the following: Thomas A. Adamich, the American Truck Historical Society, John Blachowski, Jim Blankman, Roland Boulet, Mitch Braiman of the Petersen Automotive Museum, Bruce Briggs, David S. Brooke, Charles Collins, Fred W. Crismon, Kerry Day, Skip Gill, Steve Grobl, Vance Lee, Paul Marchand, Gregg D. Merksamer, David Miller, John Montville, the National Automobile Museum at Reno, Jim Pascoe, Ray I. Scroggins, Shekell's Antique Trucks, Donald W. Siegfried, Bob Smith of Cool Cars Only, Jim Sperry, Ron Sperry, Cliff Steele, Frank Tybush, Charlie Wacker, Bernard J. Weis, Ken Wells of the Boyertown Museum of Historic Vehicles, Burton Werner, and Ed Wildanger. Several people generously contribute to a fund at San Francisco State University that supports old-truck research. We acknowledge some of the donors here: Edward C. Couderc of Sausalito Moving & Storage, Bev Davis, Gilbert Hall, Bill Hendrickson, David Kiely of ROADSHOW, James Oates, Gene

Olson, the Oshkosh Truck Foundation, Alvin Shaw, Donald Siegfried, Ray Splinter, Erol S. Tuzcu, Art Van Aken, W. T. Van Hook, Charlie Wacker, John E. Waddell, Bill West, and Fred Woods. Several chapters of the American Truck Historical Society have also provided financial support to the program at San Francisco State University. The chapters include the following: Black Swamp, Central Coast of California, Hiawathaland, Inland Empire, Mason-Dixon, Metro Jersey, Minnesota Metro, Music City, Northeast Ohio, Shenandoah Valley, South Florida, and Southern Michigan.

We should also mention the National Woody Club, which is a large and well-organized group of woody owners and fans. Several of its officers and members were helpful in the preparation of this book. The club's roster contains lists of both members and their vehicles. Interestingly, nearly half of the National Woody Club members live on the West Coast. Since this book's chapters are laid out by decades, we shall rely on the club's roster to give an indication of woodys that "survived."

This 1930s-era wagon was molded of clay.

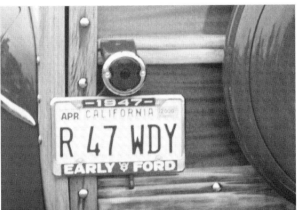

Woody owners have fun with personalized license plates.

Introduction

As with many truck and auto body styles, the station wagon can be traced back to horse-drawn days. Bruce Briggs, in his book, *The Station Wagon, Its Saga and Development*, described the development of the horse-drawn depot hack, used to carry passengers between rail or vessel terminals and hotels or resorts. During the 1890s, several other terms were used: "depot wagon," "depot Rockaway," "Rockaway station wagon" and "suburban station wagon." Some of the terms were coined as model names by specific wagon builders. Briggs described two other types: "The *Beverly* wagon, originating in the '80s, referred to a particular classification of wagon, a three-spring type—one elliptical spring parallel to the front axle, the other two mounted across the rear axle. The Beverly wagon really held to the line of our original definition [of station wagon] since it always had a removable rear seat and a drop tailgate allowing full access for loading the body, but it seldom had a top. Still another kind was the *wagonette*, whose term meant specifically longitudinal seating (passengers backed against the sides facing a center aisle with a rear entrance), like today's paddy wagon." Briggs also noted a similarity, in building the early wagon bodies and boats: ". . . unlike a boat hull, it was ribbed from the outside rather than from within. The structure of vertical and horizontal ribbing gave the outer surface a paneled appearance, not too unlike the wood station wagon body of the 20th Century."

Avon distributed men's aftershave lotion in the truck-shaped bottle shown here. The bottle is lying flat, and the plastic station wagon body lifts off. I purchased it in an antique store. On the bottom, in longhand, was written "1923 STAR."

This pair of bookends was purchased in St. Louis in the 1980s.

This is a salt and pepper set. The saltshaker is on the left. When flat, it looks like a station wagon at the bottom of the window line. The windows, roof, and surfboard are seen on the right; they hold the pepper.

American Red Ball Transit Company distributed these wooden banks.

One point needs to be made early in this book: nearly all auto manufactures produced what is known as a "commercial" chassis. These usually would consist of the auto chassis, power train, and front sheet metal back to the cowl either including or excluding the windshield. These commercial chassis would then be shipped to individual truck body builders, where they would be outfitted with delivery, ambulance, station wagon, or another form of body. Sometimes the body would be a "one-of-a-kind," or it might be one of several dozen or several hundred identical bodies built for a single buyer (or for the chassis builder himself, who might market them through his existing dealer network). Truck chassis, including light-truck chassis, were also produced and similarly delivered to body builders to be outfitted with final bodies, and then delivered to customers. Some body builders also placed unassembled bodies into "kits" that would be shipped to dealers or local body or blacksmith shops for installation. Body kits were also exported. As automakers began offering station wagons as part of their product line, they contracted with outside body builders to supply them with completed wagons in blocks of several hundred. Ford came closest to building its own station wagons.

Many firms built station wagon bodies. Some of the better-known firms were Babcock, Cantrell, Columbia, Cotton, Hercules-Campbell, Hoover, Ionia, Martin-Parry, Mifflinburg, Murray, Springfield, U.S. Body and Forging Company, Waterloo, and York. In addition, there were firms that would either build the body or install a body built by the firms listed above. Some body-building firms might build only one body, more or less custom. Sometimes, partially wrecked vehicles would be rebuilt with wooden station wagon or truck bodies because the person doing the work was more adept at working with wood than with metal.

The auto industry is now over 100 years old. The woody belongs to the first half of that century. In that first half century the auto went through many technological advances, and the auto of 1950 was far different from that of the year 1900. The wooden body, whether on a station wagon or a truck, fit more comfortably in the early part of the century. Production methods, materials requirements, and highway speeds and safety all demonstrated the need to move from wood to steel. As one studies the evolution of autos and trucks, one can see that during the first half of the twentieth century, they evolved away from the use of wood in their bodies. The woody bodies shown in this book display a form and level of detailed craftsmanship in woodworking that still can be appreciated today.

Another term—originating in England—is "shooting brake." This vehicle, initially horse drawn, and then motorized, is similar to our station wagons. It was used to carry hunters to and from the sites of their hunting.

The word "woody" also deserves some discussion. Toby Lampert wrote a good definition of the vehicles now considered woodys: "A woody is a motor vehicle built primarily between the onset of the motor vehicle age and 1953 that uses wood as an integral part of the structure or aesthetics of the vehicle. . . . Depot hacks, station wagons, and even early buses were woodys. Early wooden specialty bodies for other purposes could be considered too. Woodys were initially constructed of necessity, as wood was a familiar, readily available, and cheap material. Carriage makers were among the first auto designers, and they simply used materials that they were comfortable with. After all, the strength and durability of many species of wood was well known." Lampert also said he believed that the Industrial Revolution "provided the technology to create the automobile and at the same time provided an aversion to the mass-produced goods of the day. . . . Even then the appeal of the natural and the handmade was an integral part of the marketing strategy."

CHAPTER 1

1911–1920

The roads of the first and second decades of the twentieth century were primitive compared to modern highways. Paved roads existed only within developed areas, and virtually all passenger travel of any distance was by rail or by water. Hence, there was widespread demand for vehicles to connect passengers with rail or boat transport. In another book, *American Buses* (also published by MBI Publishing Company), I wrote about the early buses used by hotels to take guests to and from rail stations and ferry terminals. Many of these early rigs were referred to as "depot hacks," a name that would later evolve into "station wagons." These depot hacks met that early need because they could carry varying combinations of passengers and luggage. When not busy at that task, they could do other light hauling. Streetcar lines were no longer extended; motorized jitneys and buses were used instead.

Before long, private individuals required vehicles with capabilities similar to those of the depot hacks. The station wagon, especially with its removable rear seats, offered more possibilities than either a straight auto or a truck. That idea holds until today, when one can view all of the sport-utility vehicles and vans on the market and see that their respective cargo-carrying

This wooden frame-and-panel body are on a restored 1911 Buick truck owned by Edward Chatfield. Note the chain drive.

The extensive reliance on wood for framing motor vehicles is shown on this partially restored 1912 body, photographed in the Swiss Transport Museum, Lucerne.

capacity is measured in cubic feet with the rear seats both up and down.

Who built the first such vehicles? A flyer published by the Northport Historical Society in Northport, New York, said the following on that subject: "It is difficult to establish the 'originator' of the popular wooden suburban cars that came to be known to another generation as 'woodys'. . . . [An] early builder was Boston's Cotton Body Company, which produced the 1914 Ford-chassis Beverly wagon. Some historians claim that the inclusion of features of the horse-drawn Beverly of the 1880s, with its removable seats and drop tailgate, give Cotton claim to have originated the suburban station wagon."

A history of J. T. Cantrell & Company gives a different opinion: "In 1915 J. T. Cantrell and Brother built a forerunner of the station wagon on a model T chassis and called it a 'depot wagon'. . . . The depot wagon was an immediate success and the brothers were flooded with orders. This type of car filled [a] void. In 1915, Long Island and the surrounding areas outlying New York City were still largely rural. Its utilitarian concept of design, rugged quality, and [the firm's] well-established reputation from carriage building made it a logical choice for the farmer who gave up his buggy for an automobile. It combined the wagon's ability to haul loads with motorized convenience. Indeed, the term depot wagon referred to carrying goods to the train depot."

The Dodge Brothers car was popular during this era. The Martin Truck & Body Corporation of York, Pennsylvania, supplied the "Park Auto Body" to Dodge dealers. Dodge shipped the chassis with cowl to York's plant. At that time the Dodge Brothers

This is probably a used 1913 or 1914 Cadillac chassis that the Charles Wacker Wagon Builder firm of Philadelphia, Pennsylvania, used for building a funeral home's "first call" car (the one used to transport the remains in a wicker basket to the mortuary). Charlie Wacker, associated with the firm for most of the twentieth century, recalled that used auto chassis were often converted to a second use by having a new body built. Wacker said that the funeral industry had the highest demands for quality in any vehicle body supplied. He said the body consisted of an oak frame and poplar-wood panels with a fine cheesecloth lining on the inside to prevent cracking and warping. Wacker also commented that finishes then were not as good as they are today, so vehicles had to be revarnished every 18 months. *Charlie Wacker*

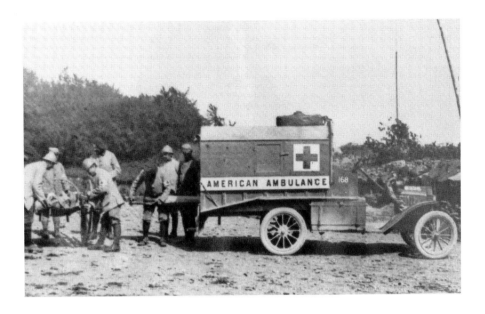

This wooden ambulance body on a circa-1914 Ford was used by the French Army during World War I. Too many soldiers sitting on the tailgate could probably tip the rig. *American Field Services*

The wooden body on this circa-1915 Ford and its passenger-carrying trailer are of matched construction. The front vehicle also has a roof, rolled-up curtains, and a luggage rack just below the roof. Note the chain drive in front of the rear wheel; the truck's frame has been extended using one of many "extendo" kits that were marketed before Ford offered TT trucks in 1917. The siding is either ship-lapped or tongue-and-grooved together. *California Highway Patrol*

This International "high-wheeler" has 1915 license plates and carries a wooden bookmobile body. *Gerstenlager Corporation*

Note the wooden shelving and doors. In the foreground are some of the bookmobile's patrons. Wooden station wagon bodies were often used as bookmobiles. The fitting of shelves and doors was probably less challenging than working with a metal body. *Gerstenlager Corporation*

commercial chassis was similar to the auto's, except that the gasoline tank was moved forward to a position under the front seat, freeing up space behind the rear axle.

This was the first decade of the Ford Model T, and its widespread use opened the possibilities of the motorcar and truck. Nearly all bodies fit to Ford commercial chassis were built of wood. In absolute numbers, in some years Ford Model T trucks outnumbered all other makes of trucks combined. And for many years there would be more Ford depot hacks and station wagons than all other makes combined.

The vast majority of truck bodies produced during this era were also made of wood or wood framing. Wood even found its role in dump-truck bodies. Wooden beams would be placed between the truck frame and the frame to which the base of the dump body was attached to cushion and protect the truck's chassis from the impact of heavy loads dropped into the dump bodies. Wood was also used at the top of the dump body's side rail to absorb the blows of steam shovel buckets. Every so often the plank would be replaced—easier than taking dents out of the steel body sides.

During World War I, many of the truck bodies built for military use were of wood. Troop carriers, ambulances, and military police (MP) "paddy wagons" used by the U. S. Army would qualify as woody wagons.

As the decade ended, Americans were ready to get into their vehicles and onto the road. Several coast-to-coast convoys were conducted to demonstrate the need for better highways. Starting in 1916, the federal government began funding highway improvements and, at the end of World War I, gave its surplus military trucks to the states to use for highway construction and maintenance. By 1920 the entire motor-vehicle industry and all its associated components were ready to "explode." The station wagon would be just one small part of a major change in the manner in which Americans lived. The tentative steps made toward building station wagons in this decade would become more positive in the following decade, when several efforts were made that qualified as "mass production."

We mentioned in the Preface that the National Woody Club has a roster of members and their vehicles. Since this book is laid out by chapters related to decades, at the end of each chapter we shall present some surviving vehicle totals, as calculated from figures in the National Woody Club's May 2000 roster. (Note that these may include a few trucks, hot rods, sedans, and convertibles with wood trim.) About the only surviving vehicles reported from 1911 to 1920 are eight Fords. (There are also a few others in museums or private collections that are not on the club's roster.)

This 1916 Ford Model T has an enclosed cab and a pickup body. Note that the body is a single unit; later, most bodies would have separate units for the cab and cargo bed to reduce problems of stress in the middle of the truck's frame. The truck was restored by B. W. Wine. *Velma Wine*

This close-up shows details of the frame and panel. The lamps on the cowl were not original. *Velma Wine*

The term "jitney" has been applied to small buses that run on semiformal schedules. This 1916 Ford with a jitney body was displayed at an auto show. A sign on the fenders calls it a "1916 Ford TT Hotel Bus," although Ford TTs (the heavier truck version of the auto) did not appear until 1917.

Just enough twigs were used to camouflage this Rolls-Royce armored car to qualify it as a "woody." It was used by the British Army in East Africa during World War I. *Public Archives of Canada*

The phrase "GMC Jitney" is painted on the side of this World War I–era rig. Its "wagonette" body is wooden, with seats on either side of the body behind the driver. *Free Library of Philadelphia*

This 1917 Hudson has a wooden, troop-carrying body. Seating in the Hudson is "wagonette" style, with seats along each side of the body. *Fred Crismon*

A wooden frame-and-panel-enclosed cab and a wooden-grain body is shown on a 1917 Oldsmobile chassis. The photo was taken at the Hays Antique Truck Museum in Woodland, California. The cab appears newer than the rest of the truck. The panels are probably plywood. The frames are fastened together by tongue-and-groove joints.

This "wagonette" seating arrangement was used on some passenger-carrying vehicles. The seats along the side could be folded to allow more room for freight. The chassis here is a 1917 Studebaker, and the words "Studebaker Ball Team" are stenciled on the trunk we see on the left. *National Automotive History Collection, Detroit Public Library*

Shown is a World War I–vintage "paddy wagon" used by U.S. Army military police (MPs). The body sides are made of a wooden frame with panels at the bottom and wire mesh at the top. It qualifies as a "woody" and as a "station" wagon, with a different type of station in mind. *Fred Crismon*

Daniel Wright, of California, and his father restored this 1919 Chevrolet with a wooden passenger body from "a pile of rusty pieces." *Daniel Wright*

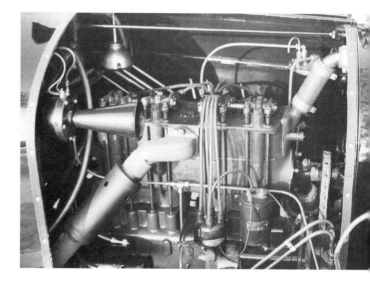

This close-up of the 1919 Chevrolet's engine shows a simpler power plant than most of us have under today's hoods. This engine could produce 22 horsepower. *Daniel Wright*

The S. S. Albright Company was a well-known body builder in the Sacramento area. This circa-1919 Dodge contains an open wooden frame-and-panel body with four rows of seats behind the driver's seat. *California State Library*

A wooden body built on a 1919 Ford chassis. Wood trim strips were applied generously. Hoover vacuum salesmen used this truck, and a vacuum was displayed behind glass. *The Hoover Company*

No. 540—WATERLOO SUBURBAN
(Patents Applied For)
The Most Popular, Best Designed, Substantially Built and Attractively Finished Suburban Body Made

Shown is a catalog picture of a Waterloo body intended for placement on a circa-1920 Ford chassis.

This is a xeroxed copy of a sheet from a circa-1919 loose-leaf catalog issued by the United Automotive Body Company, of Cleveland, Ohio. *The Ohio Historical Society*

While this truck isn't a "woody," the roadway, made of wooded poles, is. This truck was used in logging operations in the Pacific Northwest. The truck's wheels are spool-shaped with the rear wheels having some pattern inside to provide traction. *University of Washington Library*

This wooden laundry truck body was ready for placement on a truck chassis and cowl. The ladder on the side led to the roof rack, where bags of soiled laundry were placed. Slight lines barely visible on the sides and behind the seats appear to indicate that 12-inch-wide boards were used. Crown Coach built the body. Crown Coach was located in Los Angeles, California, and is known primarily for building school buses and fire apparatus. *Crown Coach Corporation*

This station wagon is being built on a 1920 Reo chassis by Frank Tybush, of New York State. About a decade ago he purchased two Reo touring cars: a 1920 model and a 1921 model. Since the 1920 models were rarer, he decided to restore that one. He wrote: "Since touring cars of all shapes, makes, and sizes are seen at almost every old car show, we decided to do an Estate Wagon body." In this picture we see that the top horizontal support is screwed and glued to the vertical framing. The small side panel is rabbeted into the vertical framing. *Frank Tybush*

This photo shows the framing on the passenger's side of the Tybush Estate Wagon. On the driver's side there will be no doors, and the left running board will hold a spare tire, the rearview mirror, and a toolbox. The curved piece of wood over the wheel was probably steamed. The less severely bent pieces were probably cut into shape using a band saw. A number of glue clamps are visible. Red oak is being used in building the body, along with red mahogany. *Frank Tybush*

Tybush made the back interior deck of oak and black powder-coated steel side ribs. The rear-framing horizontal and vertical pieces are mortise-and-tenoned together and then bolted. Reo autos were manufactured until 1935. *Frank Tybush*

Possibly built for commercial purposes, this truck body looks like it was shaped from a single log. The chassis looks like a World War I–surplus Jeffery. *American Automobile Manufacturers Association*

A flooring company displayed its abilities when finishing the exterior of this body built for promotional purposes in about 1920. The door is made of a standard mortise-and-tenoned frame. The siding is ship-lapped and the trim helps hold panels together and hide edges. *Institute of Texas Cultures*

CHAPTER 2

1921–1930

A milestone in the development of station wagons occurred in 1923 when Durant Motors' Star division ordered a batch of station wagons in advance of sale. They were delivered to the sales floors of dealers, who then attempted to sell them. This was a break from the then-usual practice of having the buyer purchase a chassis and make arrangements with a coach builder to add a station wagon body. Stars were probably the first mass-produced station wagons.

Nevertheless, some accounts hint that other body builders may have completed bodies in advance of sales even before Star started the practice. A 1974 issue of the *Long Islander* newspaper contained a history of the Cantrell firm, and said: ". . . the Cantrells would obtain a shipment of Chevy chassis, build the bodies on them and dispatch them to dealers. Then they'd begin work on Dodges. When the Dodges were finished, work would begin on another make."

The 1920s was a busy decade for the body builders—and a challenging one, because of pivotal events such as Prohibition and the beginning of the Great Depression. Anheuser-Busch had to cut back on its brewery operations because of Prohibition. Fortunately, the company already had a body-building

Two Ford Model Ts are shown in this early-1920s photo taken in Miami, Florida. The one on the right has a wooden wagon-type body that has seen some wear. Its side curtains are rolled up. What we are observing is an early version of the "Denver Boot." In the 1920s, police confiscated the seat cushions from illegally parked cars, and the miscreants would only receive their seats back when they paid their fines. The wagon is nearly full, so the police sergeant must be close to meeting his quota for the day. *Florida Photographic Archives, Strozier Library, Florida State University*

operation (which had built beer wagons and trucks for both the company and its dealers to use), so its operations were expanded to include construction of woody bodies for other companies. In Anheuser-Busch's November 1923 house organ, the *ABTatler*, was an announcement of the "Country Club" body, "designed by our president, August A. Busch, and manufactured in the body-building division of Anheuser-Busch." The bodies could fit all makes of chassis, and the *ABTatler* continued, "are ideal for the hunting or camping party. There are numerous boxes under the seats and the rear

end for carrying provisions, ice, clothing and such articles as may be found necessary for the comfort and convenience of the occupants."

At the Cantrell operation, "When a new model came out, Joseph Cantrell would design a body for it, draw up full-sized blueprints and notify dealers of the make." Salesmen traveled throughout the New Jersey, New York, and Connecticut areas, canvassing the many dealers who offered Cantrell bodies to customers.

Reo Speed Wagons were popular light or medium-sized trucks during the 1920s. In the early 1920s, Reo

The auto is probably a Ford Model T; the type of twigs used is unknown. *American Automobile Manufacturers Association*

The use of wooden siding is evident in both the truck and trailer, used by the U.S. Army Air Corps in the early 1920s. The truck is a World War I–era Liberty, and Troy built the trailer. *U.S. Air Force*

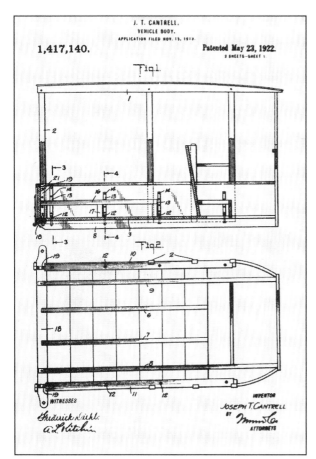

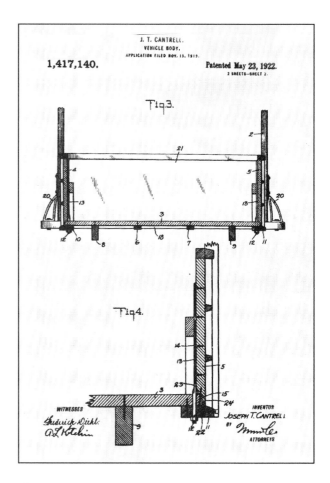

Shown are excerpts from J. T. Cantrell's 1922 patent for a vehicle body. These drawings show the entire body. *Henry D. Manwell*

These drawings show some details of construction. *Henry D. Manwell*

Here is a Crown Coach with a wagon body completed in the early 1920s. Wood was used in the top and upper sides; one cannot tell about the door panels. *Crown Coach Corporation*

A lot of timber was used to build this cabinlike structure mounted on a truck chassis that rides on rails. The rig was used in Washington State logging operations in the 1920s. Note the two-man saws carried next to the body. The water tanks above the track, made for supplying steam engines, are also built of wood. *Suzzallo Library, University of Washington*

offered two brochures that covered truck and passenger bodies available from Reo or outside suppliers. The company's truck brochure covered traveling stores, campers ("auto bungalows"), furniture bodies, and other types. One standard truck body offered by Reo was a "passenger carry-all" that had a roof, roll-up side curtains, and upholstered seats on each side of the bed, at right angles to the axles. The seats could be folded away to increase the cargo capacity, and a brochure explained that "the Carryall is formed by fitting the seats and back rests to the standard canopy top express" body. The passenger-body brochure showed many bodies that would be considered close to being "woody" wagons of that era. Most were small buses. Also shown were several pages of hotel buses, with the introductory sentence proclaiming, "The hotel hack is rapidly giving place to the fast, comfortable Speed Wagon motor bus."

In other writings about the body builders and shipment to the builder's plant for completion, the impression often given was that the body builder had but one plant. Often that is correct, and the builder served a certain geographic region. In some instances, the body builder was near one of the automakers and developed closer ties with that maker. Some body builders had a larger network. Martin-Parry, which supplied many bodies for Chevrolets and GMCs, listed the following branch assembly plants in some of their 1929 literature: Albany, Atlanta, Baltimore, Boston, Buffalo, Charlotte, Chester, Chicago, Cleveland, Columbus, Dallas, Detroit, Flint, Hartford, Houston, Indianapolis, Jacksonville, Janesville, Kansas City (Missouri), Los Angeles, Memphis, Milwaukee, Minneapolis, New Orleans, Newark, Oakland, Oklahoma City, Omaha, Oakland, Philadelphia, Phoenix, Pittsburgh, Portland (Oregon), Seattle, San Francisco, Spokane, St. Louis, Syracuse, Tarrytown, Toledo, Worcester, and York. In addition, there were Martin-Parry distributors in Allentown, Dayton, Denver, Little Rock, Pittston, Salt Lake City, Springfield (Massachusetts), and Washington, D.C. Last, there was an export office in Laredo and some relationship with the New York City office of General Motors Export Corporation. These branches could install new bodies, repair bodies

This restored 1923 Buick belongs to the Ironside family in Michigan. The body was built by Cantrell. It is constructed of white ash and has maple inserts. The spare tire appears to block the driver's door. *Louis Ironside*

The Ironside Buick's fenders are black, and the rest of the metalwork is maroon. *Louis Ironside*

of trucks that had been involved in accidents, and transfer bodies from old chassis to new chassis.

The road system was slowly improved outside of cities during the 1920s. Auto camping became popular, and people used cars (and station wagons) to carry camping and fishing gear and food for picnics. The station wagon usually had more generous cargo-carrying capacity than autos and often was believed to be slightly more "rugged" and adaptable for those outdoor expeditions.

Writing in *Special Interest Autos*, vehicle historian Michael Lamm said the following about the appeal of station wagons in the mid-1920s:

By the mid 1920s, station wagons were no longer viewed purely as utility vehicles. As the nation became wealthier and more mobile, the gentleman farmer as well as the sportsman began to recognize how handy and versatile station wagons could be. Station wagons showed up at hunt clubs and in camping caravans. Owners proudly put their monograms on the doors, as did private schools and vacation resorts. This was an era when the leisured class owned vehicles of different types for specific purposes—town cars for the opera, limousines

A look inside the 1923 Buick with the tailgate down. The two seats in the center can either be folded down or removed. *Louis Ironside*

Two lights are visible in this view from the rear. The one to the left says "STOP" and was an option. The one above the license plate says "BUICK" inside the Buick rectangular emblem and was standard equipment. *Louis Ironside*

for formal occasions, touring cars for vacations, roadsters to run around in and station wagons to take to sporting events and outings.

When Ford introduced the Model A toward the end of the decade, it began building its own station wagons (relying on a body-building firm to do some of the assembly). Lorin Sorensen wrote about the impact of Ford's decision to build its own wagons: ". . . when Ford suddenly went against the grain by introducing the industry's first mass-produced station wagon in 1929, it was the cause of some raised eyebrows. Not only because the wagon had an all-wood body that was designed to appeal mostly to the snobbish country club set, but because few in the trade could believe such a model could be built at a profit."

The real impact of Ford's decision to build its own wagons was that throughout this first half of the century,

continued on page 34

The steering wheel of the Ironside Buick is made of wood, and the windshield swings up for ventilation. *Louis Ironside*

This is a 1923 Star, photographed in the Henry Ford Museum. This was the first "mass-produced" station wagon, meaning that a batch was built ahead of orders and distributed to dealers for sale off the floor. Up until this time, station wagons were "custom" ordered, meaning the buyer would order a specific chassis and body, and the vehicle would then be completed and delivered. Star continued stocking station wagons through the 1924 model year.

The wood in this body was used to hold down tarpaper. The chassis is a 1923 Dodge, and the rig was used by a traveling theater troupe during the Depression. *National Theater Project*

Shown are the members of a motorized U.S. Army machine-gun squad, bundled up in overcoats and riding in an early-1920s White. Note the chains on the rear tires. The body is made of wood and common cabinet hardware. Its side curtains are rolled up, and there's a step at the far rear. *U.S. Department of the Interior, National Park Service, Springfield Armory National Historic Site*

This 1924 Dodge Brothers depot hack was once on display at the Imperial Palace Hotel in Las Vegas.

Anheuser-Busch once had a wagon- and body-building shop where it built equipment for delivering beer. During Prohibition, the shop began turning out other types of bodies in order to keep the work force employed. This station wagon body is shown on a circa-1924 Chevrolet chassis. *Anheuser-Busch Archives*

This Cantrell suburban body on a 1924 Dodge Brothers chassis appeared in a four-page flyer published by Cantrell. The following sentence in the flyer summed up the appeal of the suburban: "Owners of suburban homes and country estates have indeed found it invaluable for performing general utility service—for station and market use, to run out to the beach or Country Club, for hunting expeditions, for light haulage, to take children on outings, for recreation and transportation of employees—in short, to perform the many functions which mean wear and tear on a heavier, more expensive car." *Henry D. Manwell*

Ford's station wagon production was probably larger than that of all other makes combined. If one were to look at the station wagon as a social or a transportation phenomenon, one could stick with Fords and forget the rest. The rest are, however, of great interest to people interested in different types of vehicles. The coach builders' inspired use of wood on more stately chassis served to slow the sweep toward mass production.

Looking at the National Woody Club's vehicle roster, the following are the only surviving old woodys listed for the 1921–1930 decade (only those with five or more will be mentioned): 5 Chevrolets and 89 Fords.

Shown is a wooden body built on a Ford Model T chassis, probably used by itinerants. The body is decorated with license plates, antlers, and World War I helmets. Its principal license plate, mounted under the engine crank, is from California, 1927. *Special Collections, University of Arizona Library*

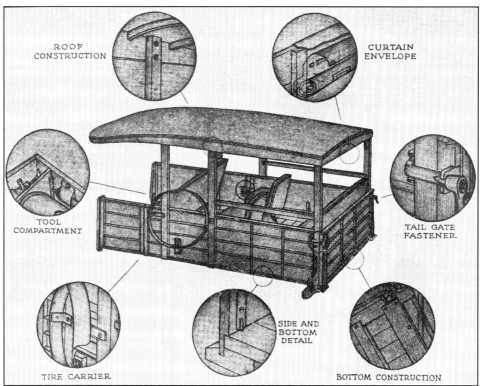

This drawing shows some of the Cantrell body's features. As the flyer said, "The great strength of the body is due to the fact that the side panels and bottom are tied together in such a way that, when a load is placed on the floor of the car, the strain does not come on the subsill, but is borne by the side panel, which is fifteen inches high. The tailgate fastener is very simple to operate and yet is practically indestructible, all parts which are liable to break being steel forgings. The specially designed tire carrier irons hold the spare tire securely in a position that is out of the way at all times. The tool compartment under the front seat makes it unnecessary to carry a metal toolbox on the running board." *Henry D. Manwell*

This photo of another Model T with a wooden body was taken in Auburn, New York, in 1929. It's decorated with only a few license plates; maybe they were used to cover leaks. *National Archives of Canada*

Note the wooden body on this early Ford TT, used by Illinois Bell for installing and servicing phones and phone lines. The cabinets are also made of wood, and the tarpaulin at the front can be drawn over the load during rainy weather. Telephone companies used large fleets of identical trucks, stocking identical equipment, so that any of the linemen would know exactly what equipment was carried. Note the solid tires; holes in the front tires are to give a more cushioned ride. The photo was taken in 1924. *Illinois Bell Telephone*

Shown is a mid-
1920s Ford TT with
a wooden cab and
stake body. The
owner was John
Bernhard, of Texas.
John Bernhard

Shown is a 1924 Ford depot hack that was once on display with the Imperial Palace collection in Las Vegas.

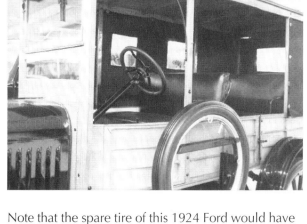

Note that the spare tire of this 1924 Ford would have to be placed on the wheel rim. It also blocks both doors on the driver's side.

This station wagon body, built in the Anheuser-Busch shops, was mounted on a mid-1920s Dodge chassis.
Anheuser-Busch Archives

The rear side curtain is down and the doors are open on the Anheuser-Busch–bodied Dodge. Note that the vehicle carries two fender-mounted, wrapped spares.
Anheuser-Busch Archives

No. 136 Convertible Estate Coachette
For Half Ton Chassis

Showing "All Weather" Enclosure drawn down.

Here is a Mifflinburg "Estate Coachette" body on a mid-1920s Ford Model T. This one is for the Ford half-ton commercial chassis. Behind the front seat are two rows of seats that can be removed. *Charlie Wacker*

No. 336 Convertible Estate Coachette
For Ton Truck Chassis

Showing "All Weather" Enclosure Open.

Here is another Mifflinburg "Estate Coachette" body on a mid-1920s Ford. This version is for the Ford TT truck chassis and the rear tire is larger (30x5 inches) than the front (30x3.5 inches). The spare-tire rack carries one tire of each size. Behind the front seat are three rows of seats that can be removed. On both models, note the angular corner panels with windows. *Charlie Wacker*

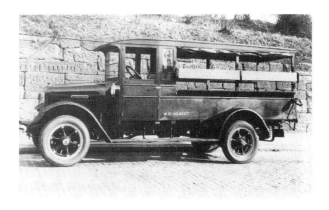

This mid-1920s International belonged to William Randolph Hearst, and it's believed to have been used at his California palace, San Simeon, to carry guests and their luggage. His guests at San Simeon included Hollywood stars and other public figures. *Navistar Archives*

This 1925 Star has a wooden depot-hack body. Bill, Sam, and Nick Clark restored it in the late 1960s. The area behind the front seat could hold passengers and freight. *Bill Clark*

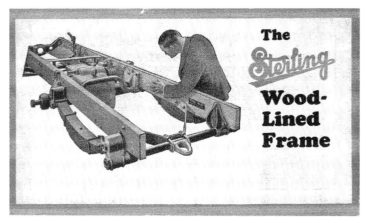

The **Sterling** Wood-Lined Frame

The Sterling Motor Truck Company of Milwaukee built medium- and heavy-duty trucks until the early 1950s. This is the cover of a brochure it issued in 1925 explaining the virtues of its wood-lined frame. The man's hand is on a 1 3/4-inch oak plank that is placed inside the frame's steel channel. Bolt holes in the frame pass through both the steel and the wood, and this includes bolts holding the engine supports, spring supports, and cross and side members. According to the brochure, the wood added strength, absorbed shocks from the road, vibrations from the motor, deadened noise, and reduced driver fatigue.

This is a 1925 or 1926 Studebaker with a Wildanger body. Note the rail a few inches above the side panels; it was added to keep children from falling out of the vehicle. The Wildanger firm was located in Red Bank, New Jersey, and was in business from 1922 to 1983. Between 1922 and 1932, the firm built about 500 wooden station wagon bodies, which it referred to as "suburban" bodies. *Ed Wildanger*

This 1926 Cadillac chassis was fitted with a Wildanger body. There are no exterior door handles because one may reach over the top of the door and operate the handle that is inside on the top of the door. *Ed Wildanger*

This 1926 Chevrolet depot hack is on permanent display at the National Automobile Museum in Reno.

Martin Parry built this 1926 hack's body.

This mid-1920s Ford TT chassis bears a passenger-carrying body with seats along each side of the bed and a rear step. It also has roll-up curtains. *Deere & Company Archives*

The spare wheel is carried next to the driver on this 1927 Chrysler with a Wildanger body. *Ed Wildanger*

Despite its popularity as a durable exterior building material, stucco never took the place of wood when it came to building station wagons. Here is one, however, used for promoting new home developments in California. Note the tiny rear door. *Whittington Collection, CSU Long Beach*

This is a restored 1927 Ford TT with a wooden school bus body. The body is more wood than metal; note the tacks holding down the roofing material. *Blue Bird Body Company*

Shown is a 1927 Hupmobile with a wooden panel body, photographed at a California Trucking Association show in the late 1970s.

This 1927 Star, with a replica of a Mifflinburg body, was on display in Los Angeles at the Petersen Automotive Museum's 1999 exhibit "Surf's Up! The Great American Woody." It's unknown whether the vehicle was originally outfitted as a depot hack. Stars were built until 1927. Bob Krause owns this woody.

This open-sided 1928 Buick Six wagon was photographed at a Christie's April 2000 auction in Tarrytown, New York. The words "Prairie Schooner" are painted on the front door. *Gregg D. Merksamer*

Shown is a 1928 Ford A depot hack that was once on display at the Imperial Palace in Las Vegas.

Richard DesRosiers owns this 1928 Dodge wagon. Note the snap-down side curtains. This wagon is painted dark red with black trim.

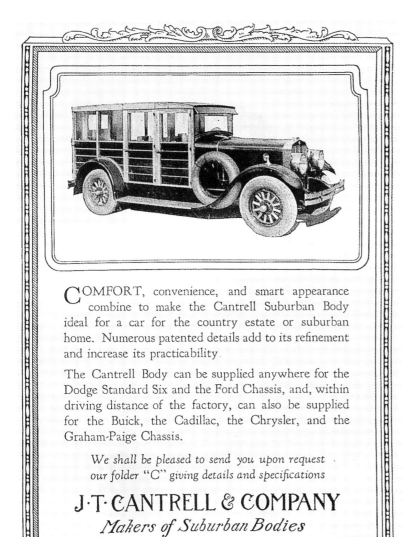

This ad for Cantrell bodies featured a 1928 Franklin. The second paragraph describes their delivery policy: "The Cantrell Body can be supplied anywhere for the Dodge Standard Six and the Ford Chassis, and, within driving distance of the factory, can also be supplied for the Buick, the Cadillac, the Chrysler, and the Graham-Paige chassis."
Henry D. Manwell

Hackney Brothers Body Company, of Wilson, North Carolina, is known mainly for its bus and refrigerated bodies. Between the two world wars, Hackney also built station wagon bodies. This is one of their in-plant photos marked up to show the differences to be incorporated into the next body built. The principal change indicated apparently is the removal of the center post and replacing it with a post between the doors and one just slightly to the rear of the rear axle.
Hackney Brothers Body Company

There's a lot of fancy wood and woodwork in this long body. It's a horse-carrying van, used by August Busch, of Budweiser fame. It's shown carrying two small- to medium-sized elephants. The chassis is a Mack AL from the late 1920s, designed primarily for intercity buses. *Anheuser-Busch Archives*

This 1928 White has a 10-passenger depot hack body. It was restored in 1980. *V. Gilbert*

This huckster body, carried on a 1928 Studebaker chassis, has wooden doors as well as a wooden truck body. *American Truck Historical Society*

Aside from the tile roof, this "productmobile" should qualify as a "woody." It was used to promote Mrs. Stover's Bungalow Candies. The chassis is a 1929 Fargo, similar to a Dodge, and was sold through non–Dodge Chrysler dealerships. *Chrysler Historical Collection*

A 1929 Ford wagon that was displayed at "Woodys on the Wharf," a woody meet held at Santa Cruz, California.

This view shows the snap-down side curtains of the 1929 Ford wagon.

Shown is a Hackney body on a Ford Model A chassis. Its side curtains are rolled up. *Hackney Brothers Body Company*

"Termite's Delight" is painted on the side panel of this customized 1929 Ford. Its metalwork is painted bright orange. The photo was taken at a 1999 auto rally in northern California.

This restored 1929 Ford AA school bus belongs to John and Sean Corr and was photographed at the Red Ribbon Car Show in Goshen, Indiana, in 1998. It's believed that the wooden body was built by the Wayne Works of Piqua, Ohio. *Gregg D. Merksamer*

Bill Gleason owns this lowered, customized 1929 Ford. The doors open toward the front.

The metalwork of Gleason's 1929 Ford is painted maroon.

This highly customized and lowered 1929 Ford's metalwork is painted bright red. The photo was taken at Wavecrest 1999. Wavecrest is an annual gathering of woodys, held in the autumn at Encinitas, north of San Diego, California.

This woody is custom-built from scraps and has a mixed parentage. The cowl is from a 1929 Chevrolet, and the fenders and grille are from a 1929 Ford. A large oxygen tank was used to roll the hood so it fit between the Ford radiator and Chevrolet cowl. A body shop in New Albany, Indiana, punched louvers in the hood and windshield visor. The body is made of oak. The engine is a Chevrolet 350-ci V-8. The builder said of the driving compartment: "You'd better like the person sitting next to you, as there is no room." *Shekell's Antique Trucks*

This customized 1929 Ford has a Chevrolet 267-ci V-8 engine and an automatic transmission. The body is handmade of oak. *Shekell's Antique Trucks*

James Wright of Colorado owns this 1929 Ford that has been rebuilt and now has a power train out of a 1987 T-Bird. It's painted aqua metallic, and many of the chromed bits have now been redone in 24-carat gold plate. Said Wright: "There is no glue at all in the wood body—everything is finger joints, lap joints, and screwed—because every piece of wood has to move." *Jim Wright*

The chassis is a 1929 White, and the photo is tagged "Huber Wagon Works of Long Island City N.Y.," the likely builder. Note the rolled-up side curtains. *Volvo/White*

This view into the rear of the 1929 White shows seats that are parallel to the axle, with cargo space behind the rear seat. *Volvo/White*

John Koll, of Colorado, owns this 1929 Oldsmobile. The body was probably built by Cantrell. Note the finished wooden wheel spokes. *Henry D. Manwell*

Shown is a Wildanger body on a 1929 or 1930 Buick chassis. On the rear door is painted in small letters "Overlook Farm." Note the single taillight. *Ed Wildanger*

Brockway trucks were built in Cortland, New York, between 1912 and 1977. Shown is a 1930 Brockway light-truck chassis with a wooden-panel delivery body that looks newly built. On the roof are extra horns and an antenna. *Roland Boulet*

This is a J. T. Cantrell & Company factory photo showing one of their bodies on a 1930 Buick chassis. The firm called this a "suburban" body. *Ed Wildanger*

Shown is a
1930 Cadillac
chassis with a
Wildanger body.
Note that the
spare tire is
not mounted
on a wheel.
Ed Wildanger

A circa-1930 Chevrolet station wagon is shown at the right, next to a large fleet of Chevrolet trucks. It was probably used for carrying employees and interplant mail and parcels. *Negea Service Corporation, Cambridge, Massachusetts*

Wooden planks were used to build this long, flared pickup body on a circa-1930 Chevrolet chassis.

This is a Hackney "Suburban" body on a 1930 Chevrolet chassis. It was completely enclosed and could seat nine (although the front seat would be a tight fit). *Hackney Brothers Body Company*

OUR No. 960—SUBURBAN BODY: Fully enclosed and an ideal passenger Bus Body for light delivery chassis. It has a capacity for 9 adults including driver and small sketch showing seating arrangement is also shown on this page. These bodies are suitable for mounting on light delivery chassis, and make an ideal station wagoner Suburban Body Equipment, as they have every convenience of a coach or sedan type body.

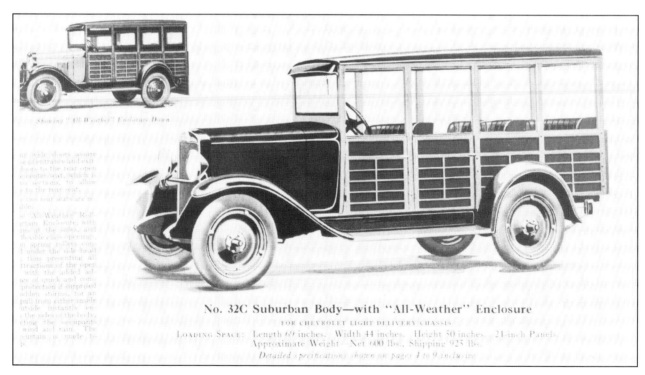

Showing "All Weather" Enclosure Down

No. 32C Suburban Body—with "All-Weather" Enclosure
FOR CHEVROLET LIGHT DELIVERY CHASSIS

LOADING SPACE: Length 69 inches. Width 44 inches. Height 50 inches. 21-inch Panels.
Approximate Weight: Net 600 lbs. Shipping 925 lbs.

Detailed specifications shown on pages 4 to 9 inclusive

This portion of a page is from a circa-1930 Mifflinburg catalog showing a wagon body for a Chevrolet chassis. The small picture in the upper left shows the side curtains down. *Blackhawk Classic Auto Collection*

This is Ed Wildanger's completed project: a dark green 1930 Ford Model A with a custom Wildanger body.
Ed Wildanger

This drawing appeared in a 1930 Standard Commercial Body Corporation booklet, showing their Suburban body on a Ford AA chassis, intended for use by the "summer hotel or country club." The description continued: "Sturdily constructed base made of selected oak with ship-lapped bottom boards. Regular equipment includes two large doors on each side fitted with curtains that operate with door, are removable and fold into pocket provided under rear seat. . . . The roof is graceful in design, close slatted with enamel duck top covering and fitted with built-in sun visor. One-piece plate glass, steel frame windshield hinged to swing in or out for ventilation. End gate in rear with short chains inside. The seats rear of driver's seat are removable. Second and third seats are halves, rear seat is a single unit. Tan art leather trimming. Spring cushions and comfortable padded backs. Wrought and malleable iron braces at points where best suited. Hand windshield wiper and outside rearview mirror regular equipment. Natural wood finish with stained panels." *Ford Archives*

Shown is a Ford Model A that has been heavily customized, lowered, and given the "flame" treatment, with a wooden panel body. It was photographed at Wavecrest 1999.

Shown is a "rogue" that showed up at a Santa Cruz woody rally. It's a 1930 Ford Model A. The headlights are not original.

This heavily customized Ford Model A and the surfboard that it carries are painted canary yellow, a color that blends well with the woodwork. The photo was taken on the Santa Cruz pier in 1999.

The body lines of the rogue show that this was probably once a delivery truck.

In 1950, *Mechanix Illustrated* magazine ran an article telling how to make an open station wagon on a Ford Model A chassis. Tom Brownell, today a well-known truck historian, used these plans to convert his 1930 Ford into this open-body woody. (Later he would add a fabric top.) Brownell had owned the Ford since he was 14 years old; it had been given to him by his uncles to use in his lawn-mowing business. Brownell's woody received a *Mechanix Illustrated* "Golden Hammer" award in 1976. The vehicle no longer exists. *Tom Brownell*

This is a 1930 Franklin with a Cantrell body. It belongs to Henry Manwell, who bought it in 1967 and then restored it with the encouragement of some of the Cantrell family. *Henry D. Manwell*

Here's a "before" picture of the cowl on Manwell's Franklin. *Henry D. Manwell*

This is the "before" picture of the disassembled body of the Franklin. It should serve as an inspiration to others considering woody restoration projects. *Henry D. Manwell*

Manwell's Franklin has snap-down curtains for both sides and the rear. Franklins were built through 1934. *Henry D. Manwell*

Shown is a rear view of a Wildanger body on a 1930 Hudson chassis. Note the side curtain pull-down tabs and snaps. *Ed Wildanger*

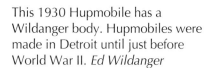

This 1930 Hupmobile has a Wildanger body. Hupmobiles were made in Detroit until just before World War II. *Ed Wildanger*

Jordan built high-class autos and was known mainly for its "Playboy" roadster model. This 1930 Jordan chassis was outfitted with a Wildanger body. Jordan production ended in 1932. *Ed Wildanger*

This interior view shows the leather upholstery and split between rear seats. This was an early use of crank-down windows, especially in the rear of wagons. *Ed Wildanger*

Graham-Paige autos were built in the late 1920s. In 1930, they were renamed; the autos were called Grahams and the taxi and commercial (light-truck) chassis were called Paiges. This picture shows a Cantrell Suburban body placed on a 1930 or 1931 Paige chassis. *Henry D. Manwell*

A St. Louis lumber company used this 1930 White for promotional purposes. It is likely that the body is built primarily of wood. *Volvo/White*

CHAPTER 3

1931–1940

Woodys of the 1930s are probably the favorites of most woody fans. Manufacturers of most makes of autos began adding station wagons to their line of vehicles during this decade. People wanting a station wagon could buy it off the dealer's floor, rather than custom ordering it through a third-party body builder. As mentioned in the last chapter, Ford built and sold the most wagons.

While the sales of station wagons were relatively low, they—and convertibles—probably helped attract floor traffic to the dealerships. Just how important having a station wagon line was to attracting general buyers is unclear, however. Over 50 years ago, I made a scrapbook of about 70 full-page new car ads that appeared in 1940 issues of *The Saturday Evening Post*. Most of them showed a single model, usually a four-door sedan. Of those ads that showed a variety of models, only two showed station wagons: Pontiac and Willys. Eight ads showed convertibles, including two (Buick and Mercury) that featured their four-door convertible sedans.

Motor camping continued to grow in popularity during this era, and the station wagon was the ideal vehicle to use. It could carry more than a conventional sedan, and its long roof could carry a canoe or small boat. If only two people were camping, they could

This 1931 Buick station wagon was photographed at the 1996 North New Jersey Antique Auto Show held in Mahwah. The body appears to be long, and it has five side windows. It may have been mounted on a longer chassis usually intended for ambulance and hearse bodies. *Gregg D. Merksamer*

A 1931 Buick station wagon similar to the one on the left. *Henry D. Manwell*

even sleep in the rear of the wagon (netting to keep out bugs could be draped over the rear). Tailgates could function as serving counters, and the idea of "tailgate parties" continues to this day; they are usually held in conjunction with football or baseball games.

The road system continued to improve, and the diligent motorist could cover several hundred miles in one day. Various government programs for creating employment helped in the development of roads and parks and other roadside attractions. Families with money preferred traveling by auto or station wagon to traveling by train. Roadside accommodations and drive-in restaurants sprang up everywhere.

Even so, the depression cut into auto production and sales. As the Cantrell company history said, "During the depression years the cars [station wagons] were not built on an assembly line basis as they were in more prosperous years. Rather, when an order came in it was assigned to one man, who undertook all phases of construction."

During this decade, catalogs were assembled and distributed to different truck and auto dealers. The dealer would also have a catalog that contained ads from various body builders who could supply and fit a body to his make of truck or commercial chassis. For Chevrolet truck buyers, the catalog was called *The Silver Book*; Hercules-Campbell, for example, ran a one-page ad in the 1938 edition for the Campbell "Suburban" station wagon body for the Chevrolet commercial chassis. It could fit either the Master or DeLuxe chassis. Dimensions were given, and all the windows were glass except for the opening over the tailgate, which was either glass or a clear curtain. Other specifications included the following: "Full width driver's seat, three-quarters width center seat and full width rear seat. Center and rear seat removable. Full width rear seat made to move up to same position as that occupied by the three-quarter center seat, if desired. Combination endgate and luggage carrier, provided with wear strips and supported by covered chains.

A view from the rear shows the 1931 Cadillac's rumble seat. A leather-covered trunk is carried on the luggage rack. *Jim Pascoe*

This is a 1931 Cadillac coupe, riding on a 148-inch wheelbase, powered by a V-16 engine. Originally it was a four-door sedan. Jim Pascoe rebuilt it with a wooden body because he was unable to find original body parts. The small door behind the right-side door is a "golf" door for a compartment intended to carry golf clubs, a feature on many sporty roadsters of that era. *Jim Pascoe*

Wood trim is used on the dash and the gearshift handle. *Jim Pascoe*

Hercules No. 3949 Station Wagon Body

FOR CHEVROLET STANDARD OR DE LUXE HALF-TON CHASSIS

LOADING SPACE—Length in Back of Driver's Seat on Floor 70″. Width 48″. Height of Side Panels 20½″. Approximate Body Weights—Net 795 lbs., Crated 1090 lbs. Approximate Weight Chassis and Body 2675 lbs. Finish—Natural Wood Varnished. CODE WORD: Scarf.

One Door on left side and two Doors on right side of Body, Storm Curtains all around and Drop Endgate with Chains, are Regular Equipment.

WE present, in this distinguish^{ed} member of the Hercules line of Better Business Bodies, a body in all ways worthy of the distinguished chassis for which it has been designed.

Price Body
$275
F.O.B. Evansville, Indiana

Featuring a wide range of usefulness, distinctive appearance, sturdy strength and comfortable seating capacity for eight adults together with generous luggage space, the station wagon body is natural wood varnished, exterior and interior, and fashioned throughout of selected wood.

All three seats and backs are padded over strong, resilient spring assembly and upholstered in a brown artificial leather to harmonize with the top and side curtain material. Rubber floor mats are provided in both compartments. Top is solid slatted over hardwood rails and covered with a heavy coated rubber-interlined fabric water-proof material, brown in color.

Side curtains are of rubber-interlined material, brown in color, with big windows. One-piece plate glass ventilating windshield. Automatic windshield wiper. Rear vision mirror. Nickel-plated door handles. The best of hardware is used throughout.

HERCULES PRODUCTS, Inc.
EVANSVILLE, INDIANA, U.S.A.

Known EVERYWHERE by this Trademark
DISTRIBUTORS IN ALL PRINCIPAL CITIES

Hercules literature for the 1931 Chevrolet half-ton chassis. The body could be placed on either the standard or deluxe chassis. *Bernard J. Weis*

AN OUTSTANDING BODY for AN OUTSTANDING CHASSIS

▼

Ideally Suited to a Wide Range of Commercial and Pleasure Uses

HERE are pictured some of the many uses to which the Hercules Station Wagon Body on the Chevrolet Standard or De Luxe Half-ton Chassis is so perfectly adapted. On a camping, hunting or fishing trip, for instance, there is ample room for the members of the party and for everything the party needs—tents, bags, fishing gear, guns, hand luggage, blankets—plus fast, comfortable transportation.

Rough roads and bad weather hold no terrors or inconveniences for the driver or passengers.

A Hercules Station Wagon Body with side curtains down, on a Chevrolet Standard or De Luxe Half-ton Chassis, furnishes dry and dependable transportation in all the services and situations in which it is employed.

The versatility of this Hercules body on the great Chevrolet chassis is further exemplified by its increasing use by county and municipal surveyors — by highway engineers and builders — in government service. By removing the two rear seats, when desired, added space for surveying instruments is quickly provided. By air ports, too, the use of this transportation unit is increasingly favored.

Its Wide Range of Usefulness Makes It an Unusually Sound Investment

TRADESMEN, who require an occasional delivery unit as well as a pleasure vehicle, find the Hercules Station Wagon Body on a Chevrolet Standard or De Luxe Half-ton Chassis ideal for quick, dependable and economical deliveries. Its smart appearance adds prestige to their business. And, whenever needed, the removal of the two rear seats provides ample space for produce and other commodities.

The Hercules Station Wagon Body on a Chevrolet Standard or De Luxe Half-ton Chassis, used as either a passenger car or a delivery unit, makes a valuable piece of delivery equipment for country clubs and estates. Resort hotels find it a good investment — as do schools, hospitals and other public and quasi-public institutions.

And on Sunday the Hercules Station Wagon Body on a Chevrolet Standard or De Luxe Half-ton Chassis, with its wide, comfortable, upholstered seats, makes a splendid car for family use and provides a speedy, good looking and comfortable means for forgetting week-day cares. Take along the picnic things, too. There's plenty of room.

HERCULES PRODUCTS, Inc.

EVANSVILLE, INDIANA, U.S.A.

Known EVERYWHERE by this Trademark

DISTRIBUTORS IN ALL PRINCIPAL CITIES

The Hercules literature described different uses for the station wagon. *Bernard J. Weis*

If one uses a larger piece of wood, one need be less concerned with matching the grain. The truck is a 1931 Chevrolet. *Clallam County Historical Society, Port Angeles, Washington*

Body finished in natural wood with harmonizing brown trim and upholstery."

The 1930s were important years for the mechanical development of motor vehicles, as well as for styling. In the 1920s, glass windows were often fitted only in the front. During the 1930s, more and more buyers opted for glass windows all around. Increased highway speeds and year-round use of the vehicles also made the snap-down canvas covers of the 1920s less desirable.

In 1935, Chevrolet introduced an all-metal wagon that shared its body with the panel truck. This would be the first coffin nail for the woody wagon, since the only advantage offered by the woody wagon was its more stylish appearance. Nevertheless, as the decade ended, most auto manufacturers still offered a wooden station wagon as part of their product line.

As more automakers offered the station wagon as part of their line, this changed the relationship between the automakers and body builders. For example, in the mid-1930s when Hercules-Campbell was making

station wagon bodies for Chevrolets (and other makes) on a one-by-one basis, they started "receiving passenger car [chassis] with windshields from the Tarrytown Chevrolet plant and shipped them off to Waterloo on transport trailers where the wooded bodies were installed and the assembled car then returned. . . . After a final inspection and a few adjustments, the dealer to whom each car was assigned from the Hercules-Campbell plant would pick it up for delivery to his customer. Dealers came from as far as California." In 1940, Chevrolet offered a station wagon as part of its line, and Hercules-Campbell became Chevrolet's exclusive supplier of wagon bodies. Now, the "bodies were completely finished and shipped in freight cars, eight per car, with equipment of special racks and tie-downs to all Chevrolet plants, three freight cars per day, five days a week." Final assembly took place at the individual Chevrolet plants.

Not everybody admired the wooden wagons during this era. Don Butler wrote that the woodys "bore the brunt of many unkind jokes and monikers. Some

No. 36 STATION WAGON BODY
—with Window Regulator and Glass in all Doors
FOR CHEVROLET STANDARD OR DE LUXE HALF TON CHASSIS

NO. 35 SAME AS 36 EXCEPT DOORS REAR OF DRIVER'S SEAT ARE EQUIPPED WITH
SNAP ON CURTAIN INSTEAD OF WINDOW REGULATOR AND GLASS.

Length rear driver's seat 70 inches. Width 50 inches with small wheelhouse. Height 50 inches.
Height of panels outside 27 inches and inside 22 inches. Finished in natural wood varnish. Accommodates 8 persons with ample space for luggage on the lowered end gate.

Approximate Weight—Net 750 lbs., Shipping 1190 lbs.

Painting hood and cowl brown extra

List Prices F.O.B. Mifflinburg, Pa. No. 36—$350.00. No. 35—$335.00

No. 36 Can also be furnished with removable glass frame or window regulator and glass in side
opposite rear seat instead of snap-on curtain at an extra cost.

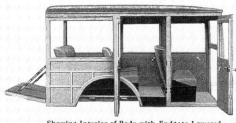

Showing Interior of Body with Endgate Lowered.

Illustrating the "Weather-Tight" Storm Curtains.

FOUR 28-inch doors assure an ease of entrance and
exit. On the No. 35 the right and left doors at
the driver's seat are sedan type equipped with a window regulator and glass to slide in felt channels. The
two doors rear of the driver's seat on No. 36 are also
equipped with window regulator and glass.

The weather-tight storm curtains are of the snap-on
type as shown on cut at left.

The doors to the rear open at the center seat, which
is in two sections, to allow access to the rear seat.
The two rear seats can be removed, thus converting
the body from a passenger car to a delivery unit,
which makes the car a valuable addition to the equipment of Country Clubs and Estates.

The cushions and backs are deep and very comfortable. The floor of the body is equipped with
rubber mat easily removable. The body is equipped
with slanting VV plate glass windshield, automatic
windshield wiper, rear vision mirror and nickel plated
door handles, also adjustable inside sun visors above
driver's seat which can be dropped to desired position.

THE MIFFLINBURG BODY CO.
MIFFLINBURG, PA.

This ad shows Mifflinburg bodies for 1931 Chevrolets. Two body styles were offered, and the only difference
between the two was whether windows behind the front seat were glass or used snap-down curtains. The
glass-version body cost $350; the one that used curtains cost $335. *Bernard J. Weis*

In March 1932, the U.S. Army took delivery of this station wagon built on a 1931 Ford Model A chassis.
Fred Crismon

This very common wooden body was used on Ford Model AA mail trucks built for the U.S. Postal Service. This 1931 version was for sale at a Scottsdale auction in early 1999.

wagon owners were asked: 'Why don't you take the rest of your car out of the shipping crate?' A cruel observation suggested that 'it would look better if sheet metal covered the bare wood framework.' It was sometimes called a 'lumberjack's dreamboat' and the less complimentary 'sawmill surrey' was also heard. Most slanderous of all was the reckless remark that the wagon was a 'woodpile with wheels.' Despite these occasional barbs from the balcony, the wooden wagon stayed onstage and went on working its way to stardom."

The National Woody Club's roster shows that many woodys survived from the decade 1931–1940. Totals (greater than four) include 15 Buicks, 20 Chevrolets, 479 Fords, 6 Internationals, 13 Packards, 21 Plymouths, and 15 Pontiacs. Note the overwhelming number of Fords; there were 85 1939 Fords and 137 from 1940 on the list. After World War II, late-1930s Ford wagons became popular with both surfers and collectors.

This customized 1931 Ford belongs to John Beradon.

The area behind
the 1931 Ford's
front seats is
clear and neat.

This early-1930s International chassis carries a Hackney body. Note how narrow the seat back above the rear axle is, compared with the back of the front seat. *Hackney Brothers Body Company*

This 1932 Cadillac is carrying a Wildanger body. *Ed Wildanger*

SEMI-SEDAN MODEL—
The ideal car for station work or shopping, taking children to school, moving small pieces of furniture, and the hundred and one odd jobs of transportation that no other car can do satisfactorily. Rich in appearance, speedy, easy to handle, the Studebaker-Cantrell Suburban will appeal to you from every standpoint.

CONVERTIBLE MODEL—
This body has all of the good features of the semi-sedan model combined with complete rough weather protection. The glass in the driver's doors are moved up or down by means of window regulators while the removable sashes are held in place with screws. The curtains for use in summer are left on while the sashes are in use.

STUDEBAKER SUBURBAN SIX

The interior of this Cantrell flyer shows the company's bodies on 1931 Studebaker commercial chassis. The literature said: "The Studebaker Cantrell Suburban may be had in three different models, the curtain, the semi-sedan [shown on right] and the convertible [shown on left]. The first model is furnished with curtains for all openings. Those for the doors open with the doors. The semi-sedan is equipped with glass in the front doors, curtains being used in all other openings. The convertible model is a semi-sedan furnished with extra sashes for the side openings. These sashes are screwed in place in the fall, and left in during the winter months. This model gives the best protection in bad weather." *Henry D. Manwell*

Shown is a side view of a 1932 Chevrolet with a Cantrell body. *Burton Werner*

Cantrell Suburban Bodies have been building good will among dealers and users since 1915. They are not only on the estates of many of the best known people of America, but are also in use in most foreign countries including France, England, Ireland, Russia, Sweden, and the Hawaiian Islands.

Wherever distinction as well as long wearing qualities are required, Cantrell Suburbans will be found. They are built by a company that has specialized in this type of body and it is natural that they should have developed, over a period of years, a sturdiness, comfort and refinement that cannot be found in any other body.

The basic patented mechanical design ties the side panels, sub-sills and floor together in such a way that the load does not put a strain on the sills and sub-sills alone, but is carried by the side panels. It is obviously impossible to deform or break this 3/4" panel standing on edge. The panels are of solid 3/4" cottonwood and the trim is Quartered Red Gum. The posts, carlines, sills and sub-sills are of White Ash, of the best grade, and the floor is hard Pine.

The great care taken in the design of this body is shown by the fact that practically all of the malleable irons, such as strap bolts and top braces, are of Cantrell design. It will be noticed that comparatively few of these irons are used, as the fundamental design of the body insures great strength without the use of heavy irons.

The tailboard is securely fastened by means of our patented swinging bolt and nut fastener, which ties the tailboard to the panel in such a way as to prevent any possibility of rattle. It is easy to operate and practically indestructible. The doors are wide and are fitted with sturdy and good looking hardware. All doors are fitted with dovetails and rubber bumpers.

The body is designed to carry seven passengers comfortably, though in the regular models, only two full width seats are furnished. A pair of aisle seats can be had at an additional cost of $25.00. Seats back of the driver's are readily removable, thus giving unobstructed floor space of 72" x 46½".

Great care has been taken to have all seats comfortable. They are stuffed with real curled hair and furnished with deep springs. The covering is of Chase artificial leather which we have found to compare favorably in wearing qualities with real leather. The design of this leather is distinctive and harmonizes perfectly with the natural wood finish of the body.

The roof construction gives a smooth surface which is very desirable as it means long wear. The deck itself is waterproofed composition board and is covered with rubberized deck material. The side curtains are of sport material and are hung inside the top rail in such a way that when not in use they are not exposed to the weather. Lift-the-dot fasteners are used throughout. The floor is covered with a rubber mat.

The Cantrell Suburban can be had in two models. The semi-sedan which is furnished with drop windows in the driver's doors only and the convertible sedan which is furnished with drop windows in the driver's doors and stationary removable glass sashes in all other side openings. This model is also furnished with the same curtain equipment as the semi-sedan model and is an all-weather job, as it can be used as a sedan model during the winter months and converted into a semi-sedan for the summer.

LIST PRICES AT HUNTINGTON, N. Y.

Semi-Sedan $347
Weight Crated 1030 lbs.

Convertible Sedan $405
Weight Crated 1080 lbs.

Prices include mounting at Huntington. If body is to be shipped, add $20.00 for crating.

J. T. CANTRELL & COMPANY
HUNTINGTON, L. I., N. Y.

This ad shows Cantrell bodies for fitting onto 1932 Chevrolet chassis. Two bodies were available: one with glass windows and one with some side curtains. Prices included mounting at Cantrell's Long Island plant. *Bernard J. Weis*

CAMPBELL DE LUXE STATION WAGON BODY

With glass in two front doors
and curtains on balance

$360.00

Mounted or crated. Tarrytown
Extra for full glass on sides,
curtain in rear, $68.00

Campbell De Luxe Station Wagon Body
For Chevrolet Standard or De Luxe Half-ton Chassis

FOR years Campbell has been designing Station Wagon Bodies to meet the ever increasing demand for a suburban body of character, incorporating the newest ideas of the day, and thousands are now in use on estates, country clubs, etc.

Herein he presents his latest creation in which you will find the very best features born of his experience plus a brand of master craftsmanship developed in his organization through years of continuous building.

Above is shown the CAMPBELL DE LUXE STATION WAGON BODY. The sloping windshield, streamline top and curved rear blend with the harmonious tone of color in the perfectly matched maple of the body. The color combination yields a rich and distinctive effect, expressing ultrasmartness. The body accommodates six passengers and chauffeur in comfortable form-fitting seats.

At the right is shown the automatic lock-tight combination End-Gate and Luggage Carrier, covered with three wear strips and supported by fully covered chains. The three-quarter center seat, accommodating two, permits easy access to rear seat, and by eliminating dangerous left rear door, body rigidity is retained — both rear seats are easily removed.

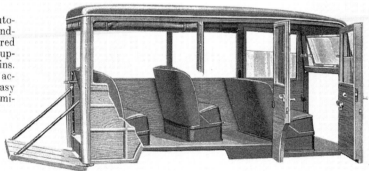

HERCULES-CAMPBELL BODY COMPANY, Inc.

TARRYTOWN, N. Y., Telephone: Tarrytown 1117 and 1118

Albany, N. Y. Branch	Portland, Me. Branch	Cambridge, Mass. Branch
Tivoli Street, Tel: Albany 3-1523	St. John Street, Tel: Preble 1275	27 Tudor Street, Tel: Porter 5270 and 5271

In 1932, Hercules-Campbell offered these bodies for Chevrolet standard and deluxe half-ton chassis. The lower drawing shows that the center seat mounts to the left, with space on the right. There is no rear door on the left side. *Bernard J. Weis*

All doors are supported by continuous hinges; the two front doors are fitted with full plate windows operated by regulators. Sides and rear are equipped with Quick-Drop curtains, as illustrated.

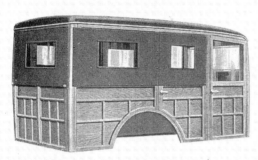

Quick-Drop tailored weather-tight curtains, fastened in place, providing ample vision.

Glass enclosed model with windows set in felt channels and operated by quick-acting regulators. Over end gate there is a drop-curtain; glass is available for this section at extra cost.

Campbell DeLuxe Station Wagon Body Specifications

Full width driver's seat, three-quarter width second seat and full width rear seat. Second and rear seats removable.

Front and rear floor mats.

Full vision, one-piece plate glass windshield in chromium plated steel frame with automatic windshield wiper. Rear vision mirror.

Continuous hinged doors, the two front doors equipped with full plate windows operated by quick-acting regulators. Also equipped with remote door controls.

Automatic lock-tight combination End-Gate and Luggage Carrier, covered with three wear strips and supported by covered chains.

Body finished in Pure Maple with harmonizing Brown trim and upholstery.

INSIDE BODY DIMENSIONS

Height 47″ under bows.	Height of side panels (outside) 26¼″.
Width 50″.	
Length 70″ behind driver's seat.	Width of front doors 26½″.
Height of side panels (inside) 21″.	Width of side doors 28¾″.

Glass enclosures for side and rear can be furnished at extra cost.

▼

HERCULES-CAMPBELL BODY COMPANY, Inc.

TARRYTOWN, NEW YORK   Telephone: Tarrytown 1117 and 1118

Albany, New York Branch   Portland, Me. Branch   Cambridge, Mass. Branch
Tivoli St., Tel: Albany 3-1523   St. John St., Tel: Preble 1275   27 Tudor St., Tel: Porter 5270 and 5271

These Hercules-Campbell drawings show the available window options. *Bernard J. Weis*

Designed for the Chevrolet Half-Ton Chassis.

THE YORK-HOOVER
Estate Suburban Body

THERE is a very definite need for the Estate Suburban as built by York-Hoover. The real dignity incorporated in the body design places it outside the so-called "truck" designation into the passenger vehicle classification.

For the countless summer tasks of the country estate, or the carrying of equipment to that favorite fishing hole, or carrying the family to the bathing beach, or for a hundred and one other duties this type car is invaluable.

To ride in it is a mark of distinction. To own it is a real economy.

Note particularly in reading the specifications, which follow, how simple and how efficient is the method of enclosing the body. No side curtains with which to bother, merely the turn of a neat crank regulator or the simple sliding of snug metal bound windows. This is a real development in York-Hoover's Estate Suburban.

But read the specifications:—

YORK-HOOVER BODY CORPORATION

Factories and Main Offices . . . . YORK, PA.

York-Hoover Body Corporation issued this two-page flyer describing the body that it would fit to a 1932 Chevrolet half-ton commercial chassis. *Bernard J. Weis*

THE YORK-HOOVER
Estate Suburban Body
(Continued)

THERE are four wide doors, sedan type, equipped with windows that slide in felt channels and which are raised or lowered by window regulators. The two side panels next to the four doors have glass enclosures. The lower half of these enclosures is stationary, forming a rigid, vibrationless type of construction. The upper half is set in a steel frame and can be lowered 9¼″.

The passenger compartment length is 72″ on floor. The width is 49″ and the height is 49″. The front and rear seats are the full width of the body. The two center seats are 17½″ wide with a 10″ center aisle permitting access to the rear seat. This arrangement comfortably seats seven or eight passengers without crowding. The seats and back rests are upholstered in a rich shade of brown Spanish Art leather which harmonizes with the exterior finish. The seats rear of the driver are easily removed to accommodate baggage or other articles to be carried. The rear is equipped with a drop end gate and there is a roll-up curtain which is fastened to the rear posts and tailgate. A glass enclosure is obtainable if desired instead, at a nominal additional charge. The roof is covered with a drab colored guaranteed waterproof composite duck material. The floor is covered with attractive linoleum rear of the driver and in front of the driver there is a rubber floor mat. The exterior side panels are finished in walnut stain by a process which insures a lasting finish for the entire life of the body. The windshield is the full ventilator type and is hung on piano hinges at top and is supported by quadrant arms when open. Rear view mirror and automatic windshield wiper are regular equipment.

Domestic Shipping Information

The Estate Suburban body can be mounted on the chassis at York, Pa., or knocked down for shipping.

Net weight of body, approximately 890 pounds.

Weight of body crated, approximately 1100 pounds.

Approximate size of crate, 122″ long, 66″ wide, 32″ high.

For export information, write direct to York, Pa.

YORK-HOOVER BODY CORPORATION

Factories and Main Offices　.　.　.　.　YORK, PA.

The York-Hoover literature emphasized that glass windows were used all around rather than side curtains.
Bernard J. Weis

The front end of the 1932 Chevrolet looks more like a 1931 model, but owner Burton Werner believed "these parts may have been left over from the '31, and the Chevrolet factory used them for this chassis." *Burton Werner*

Looking inside the right rear door we see how far back the front seat is placed on Werner's 1932 Chevrolet. *Burton Werner*

The rear side curtains are shown rolled up on Werner's Chevrolet. The center seat is split in the middle to provide access to the seat far in the rear. *Burton Werner*

The tailgate of Werner's Chevrolet is shown in the down position, held by covered chains on each side. *Burton Werner*

The tailgate is up in this view of Werner's Chevrolet, secured by a latch on each side. There is also a rolled-up curtain for the rear. *Burton Werner*

This 1932 Ford, photographed on the pier at Santa Cruz, belongs to Al Engel.

This 1932 Ford wagon has black fenders, with the remainder of the metal bodywork painted creamy tan. *Cool Cars Only*

This view from the front of the 1932 Ford wagon shows how its spare mounts in the fender well on the passenger's side, carrying a rearview mirror on top. *Cool Cars Only*

Looking up the pillar between the doors of the 1932 Ford wagon, we see the wooden interior of the roof. *Cool Cars Only*

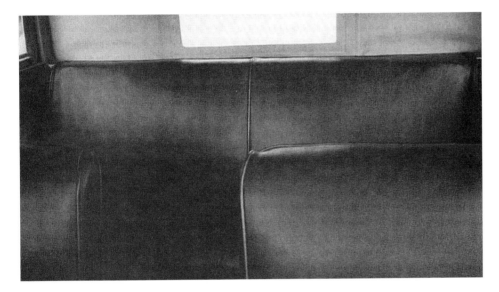

Looking back from the driver's seat of the 1932 Ford wagon we see that the middle seat is split, allowing access to the seat in the far rear. *Cool Cars Only*

The lowered tailgate of the 1932 Ford wagon is held by two covered chains. *Cool Cars Only*

This is Andy and Melodie Ohmits' customized 1932 Ford.

A rear view of Ohmits' Ford.

This 1932 Ford looks original and in need of restoration.

This 1932 Ford was
photographed at
Santa Cruz.

Here's a highly customized 1932 Ford, powered by a V-8 engine.

No external door hardware is visible on the customized 1932 Ford. It is owned by Larry Anderson, of Idaho.

Shown is a 1932 Plymouth commercial chassis with a Cantrell body. The original caption referred to this as the Cantrell "Suburban" body. The center seat is split in the middle. *Baker Library, Harvard University*

LOADING SPACE:

Length 69"
Width 44"
Height 50"
Panels 21"

This is a picture of a 1932–1933 GMC that appeared in a "Mifflinburg Custom-Built Commercial Bodies for G.M.C." booklet that was published and distributed as a bulletin by the General Motors Export Company. A smaller picture showed the wagon with its curtains down. Other body styles offered in the bulletin included panel delivery, canopy express, screen delivery, pickup, and stake. *National Automotive History Collection, Detroit Public Library*

This is a late-1932 Ford V-8 wagon owned by Fred Montanari, which was photographed in Connecticut in September 1998. Its front end is slightly different from most Fords of this era; the headlights and headlight bar are lowered. The vehicle's metalwork is painted creamy tan. *Gregg D. Merksamer*

Shown is a Wildanger station wagon body on a stately 1933 Cadillac chassis. *Ed Wildanger*

Shown is a 1933 Chevrolet station wagon, with snap-down side curtains, followed by a 1934 Chevrolet station wagon, both used by the U.S. Army. They are participating in motorized maneuvers and must be refueled by civilian tank trucks. *Fred Crismon*

This 1933 Ford is being used by an oil exploration party near Wadi Ansab, Lebanon. It has oversized tires, necessary for desert operations. The photo was taken in 1936. Note the birds tethered to the poles on the right side of the picture; their role in oil exploration is unknown. *Aramco*

Shown is a stylish Wildanger body on a 1933 Ford chassis. The author asked Ed Wildanger, of the wagon-building family, why one would buy a "custom" station wagon body on a Ford when it was also possible to buy a "regular" Ford station wagon offered by Ford dealers. Mr. Wildanger's response was that it was a form of "snob appeal," the buyers wanting others to know that they could afford something more than the "common" body. The Wildanger firm built more bodies for Fords than for any other make of chassis, building 25 Ford bodies at a single time and installing them on chassis supplied by dealers. *Ed Wildanger*

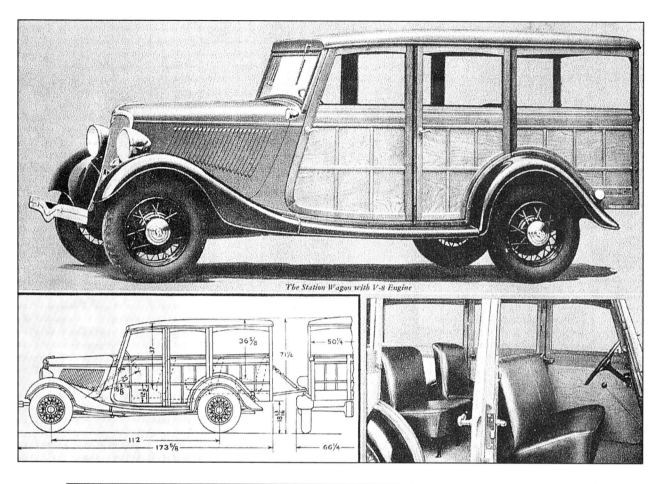

The Station Wagon with V-8 Engine

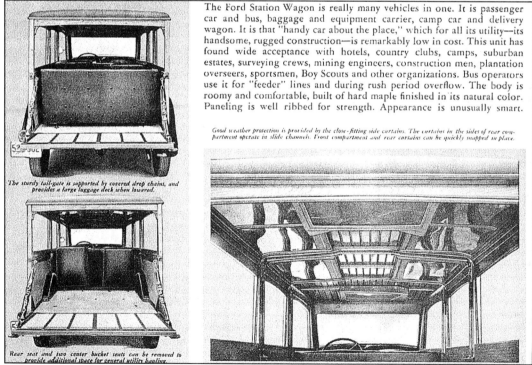

The sturdy tail-gate is supported by covered drop chains, and provides a large luggage deck when lowered.

Rear seat and two center bucket seats can be removed to provide additional space for general utility hauling.

The Ford Station Wagon is really many vehicles in one. It is passenger car and bus, baggage and equipment carrier, camp car and delivery wagon. It is that "handy car about the place," which for all its utility—its handsome, rugged construction—is remarkably low in cost. This unit has found wide acceptance with hotels, country clubs, camps, suburban estates, surveying crews, mining engineers, construction men, plantation overseers, sportsmen, Boy Scouts and other organizations. Bus operators use it for "feeder" lines and during rush period overflow. The body is roomy and comfortable, built of hard maple finished in its natural color. Paneling is well ribbed for strength. Appearance is unusually smart.

Good weather protection is provided by the close-fitting side curtains. The curtains in the sides of rear compartment operate in slide channels. Front compartment and rear curtains can be quickly snapped in place.

These pages appeared in Ford commercial car literature.

This 1933 Ford was spotted at Wavecrest 1999. It looks complete and in good shape for its age. Its color is a faded tan.

Tom Gardner's 1933 Ford has been modified considerably.

Gardner's Ford is powered by a hot-rod V-8 engine.

A Rolls-Royce adds class to any event. This 1933 Rolls "shooting brake" (a British term for vehicles used to transport hunters) was originally built for use on a Scottish estate and is shown at the Greenwich, Connecticut, Concours held in June 2000. *Gregg D. Merksamer*

This 1934 Dodge was built for the U.S. Army. Note the number of snaps holding the side curtains. *Fred Crismon*

Shown is a circa-1934 Dodge with a Westchester body. The spare tire is carried in the front wheel well. *A. L. Hansen Manufacturing Company*

If owning a station wagon gives one status, owning this 1934 Pierce-Arrow would give one "super" status. The body was built by Cantrell, and the photo was taken in 1989. Its hood was painted creamy tan, and its fenders were painted chocolate brown. Pierce-Arrow autos were built until 1938. *Bernard J. Weis*

Two U.S. Army 1934–1935 Chevrolet wagons with grille guards are shown while being refueled. *Fred Crismon*

This 1935 Chevrolet is not a woody. Instead, its sides are made of metal although its top is of composition material. The body style is similar to that of a woody, although it was shared with the panel delivery body on a light-truck chassis. Truck manufacturers and body outfitters began offering this style of body, which had the same capacity and usefulness as a wooden station wagon, but the body itself required less maintenance. (As this book is being written, a similar Chevrolet is being featured in some of Chevrolet's television commercials.) *American Automobile Manufacturers Association*

Two Fords from the mid-1930s, a station wagon and a stake truck, are shown operating on rough terrain, the Navajo Trail in Utah. *Baker Library, Harvard University*

A gray 1935 Ford wagon with white sidewalls is shown in a Santa Cruz motel lot, the night before a station wagon meet.

This 1935 Ford belongs to Art Fertin. It has been customized and is powered by a Chevrolet 350-ci engine.

This is a rear view of Art Fertin's 1935 Ford.

These are the markings on the front door of the 1936 Dodge Westchester. The front doors have glass windows. All windows to the rear have snap-on windows. Richard DeLuna owns this woody, and he was once a Santa Cruz lifeguard. He purchased the wagon from the Harrah's collection in 1984.

Santa Cruz, California, is known for its beaches and surfing and is the "capital" of woody station wagon fans and collectors. This is a 1936 Dodge Westchester, with its body built by U.S. Body and Forging Company; it has been made to look like the lifeguard wagon used in Santa Cruz over 50 years ago. It's more or less the "dean" of the Santa Cruz wagons and has been pictured in several books.

DeLuna's wagon is well traveled. Here we see it in a 1996 photo taken in New York City at the Louis Vuitton Classic, held at Rockefeller Center. On the left is a 1941 Ford owned by Malcolm Pray that won the best car trophy in the Saks Fifth Avenue "Land Yachts and Skiffs" category, and on the right is a 1948 Mercury wagon owned by Robert Akin. *Gregg D. Merksamer*

This 1935 International station wagon was used in the movie industry. Moving-picture cameras were mounted on a platform that extended in front of the chassis and on the roof. *Navistar Archives*

This 1937 Buick with a Wildanger body has glass windows all around. *Ed Wildanger*

This heavily customized 1937 Chevrolet was photographed at Wavecrest. Whether this was always a station wagon is uncertain. The encyclopedic *Great American Woodies & Wagons* by Donald Narus makes no mention of 1937 Chevrolet wagons on auto chassis.

This 1937 Terraplane wagon has three seats and carries luggage on the tailgate. Nineteen thirty-seven was the last year that Terraplanes were sold; in 1938 they became Hudson Terraplanes. *Baker Library, Harvard University*

The chassis delivered to the station wagon body outfitter came with varying configurations with regard to how far back the chassis sheet metal would extend. In this circa-1937 Studebaker chassis, the chassis builder supplied the two front doors and roof overhead, as well as the rear fenders. The station wagon body builder would need to supply the rest. Note that this chassis has right-hand steering; it was intended for export. *Smithsonian Institution*

A Wildanger body mounted on a 1938 Buick is shown here. The rear side and rear windows are covered by snap-down curtains. *Ed Wildanger*

This is a 1938 Buick Century with a Wildanger body. Its initial owner bought three Buick station wagons with Wildanger bodies at the same time, all for use at the family summer home. This one has been restored. It was originally painted tan but now is bright red. *Ed Wildanger*

Originally, this was a 1938 Buick Roadmaster four-door sedan. Jim Pascoe rebuilt it with a station wagon body, using both oak and walnut. Note that the front doors open to the front. *Jim Pascoe*

This rear view of Pascoe's 1938 Buick shows the twin taillights. Its body proportions, when viewed from the rear, seem lower and wider than one would associate with 1938 Buicks. *Jim Pascoe*

Here we see the 1938 Buick's tailgate down and the rear of the back seat. *Jim Pascoe*

This is a 1938 Chevrolet with a Campbell "Suburban" body, built by Hercules-Campbell. *The William F. Harrah Automobile Foundation*

This 1938 Dodge light-truck chassis with cowl is ready to be delivered to a truck or station wagon body builder. In this case, the body builder would have to supply the windshield and everything else behind. *Free Library of Philadelphia*

A 1938 Ford V-8 wagon with white sidewalls is shown as it arrives on a trailer at the Santa Cruz pier.

While this 1938 Ford wagon carries no surfboard, it does have a Hawaiian street sign in its side window.

This well-preserved 1938 Ford wagon was photographed at Wavecrest 1999.

Harry and Phoebe Linden own this 1938 Ford, photographed on the Santa Cruz pier.

Shown is a 1938 Plymouth wagon with a covered luggage-carrying rack on top. *American Automobile Manufacturers Association*

Bernhard Rasmussen, of New York, is the second owner of this 1938 Plymouth Westchester. In the past decade the vehicle underwent a "body-off" restoration. *Bernhard P. Rasmussen*

We see the rear end opened on Rasmussen's Plymouth. The vehicle is painted stone beige, an original color that was found under a part of the wooden body during the restoration. *Bernhard P. Rasmussen*

Here's a view inside the right rear door of the Rasmussen Plymouth.
Bernhard P. Rasmussen

This view looks toward the rear of the interior of Rasmussen's Plymouth. The center seat accommodates two; the far rear seat, three.
Bernhard P. Rasmussen

The left hood is up on Rasmussen's Plymouth.
Bernhard P. Rasmussen

Wood was widely used for building bus bodies, especially school bus bodies. This picture, taken outside a school in Iowa about 1939, shows nine buses waiting to pick up children. The dates of the chassis range from about 1927 through 1937. Only the middle chassis (with the word "Tipton") appears to be of metal construction; the other eight are of wood. *State Historical Society of Iowa*

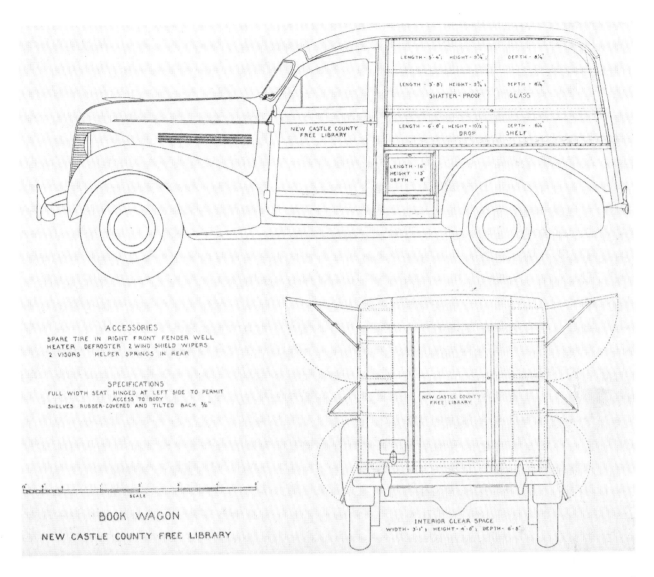

BOOK WAGON
NEW CASTLE COUNTY FREE LIBRARY

This is a drawing for a bookmobile body to be built on a 1939 Chevrolet station wagon body, for use in New Castle County, Delaware. Its rear windows swing upward to give access to books. *American Library Association*

This photo shows the completed bookmobile, which was outfitted in Wilmington, Delaware. The total cost in 1939 was $1,178. *American Library Association*

Above: This view from the rear shows that the back side windows of Larsen's Chevrolet are snap-down canvas. The only major items replaced were the running-board rubber and the roof rubber. The fenders and top are painted black, the remainder of the body is painted gray, and the wheels are painted red. *Kris Larsen*

Kris Larsen, of Massachusetts, is the second owner of this 1939 Chevrolet, mounted on a half-ton chassis. Larsen believes the body was custom-built, rather than produced by firms that regularly outfitted Chevrolet light-truck chassis at that time. *Kris Larsen*

This 1939 Chevrolet light-truck chassis was fitted with a Mifflinburg body. *A. L. Hansen Manufacturing Company*

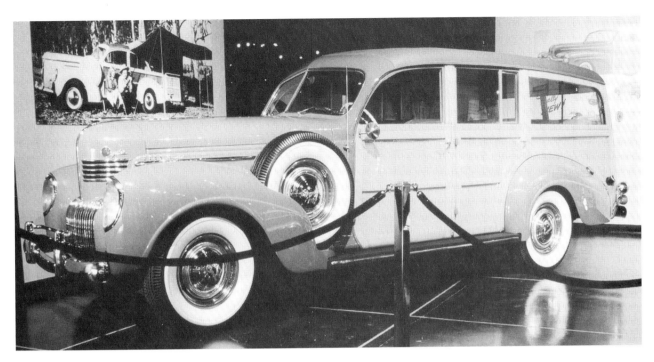

Bohman & Schwartz outfitted this 1939 Chrysler Imperial with a station wagon body. Current owner Wes Aplanalp loaned it to the Petersen Automotive Museum for its 1999 display. According to the museum, "Pasadena-based coachbuilder Bohman & Schwartz was commissioned to design and construct the body, which featured maple panels with sealed edges and joints that were glued, screwed and mortised for added strength. The body structure was further reinforced with forged iron braces." The belt line was 2 inches lower than on standard Chrysler autos in order to improve visibility.

You know that you're not in Kansas anymore when you see a wagon like this! It's a 1939 Delahaye shooting brake, owned by Klaus Werner.
Gregg D. Merksamer

The 1939 Delahaye is shown at the entrance to the Channel Gardens at the 2000 Annual Louis Vuitton Classic held at New York City's Rockefeller Center.
Gregg D. Merksamer

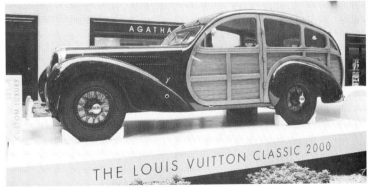

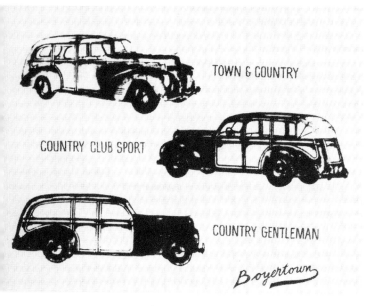

STATION WAGON
1939 — 112-inch wheelbase 4x2 Station Wagon

Boyertown Body Works submitted this drawing to Chrysler Corporation showing three wagon proposals on 1939 Dodge chassis. One model was called the "Town & Country," and some writers believe that this is where the phrase originated. *Boyertown Museum of Historic Vehicles*

The Royal Canadian Air Force used this 1939 Canadian Ford station wagon during World War II. *Fred Crismon*

Mumford's 1939 wagon is painted navy blue.

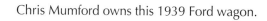

Chris Mumford owns this 1939 Ford wagon.

Hanlon's wagon is painted bright red.

Bill Hanlon owns this 1939 Ford, which now has a Chevrolet 350-ci engine.

This 1939 Ford
DeLuxe was
photographed at
Wavecrest 1999.

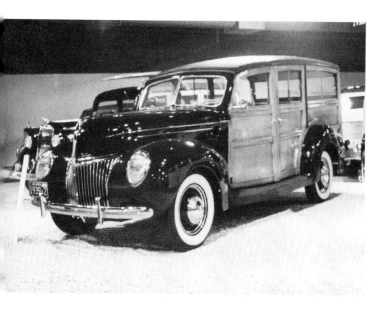

This drawing from the Navistar Archives was made just before World War II and shows the Gatti African Expedition led by two International station wagons. *Navistar Archives*

Al Bernhard loaned this 1939 Ford DeLuxe station wagon to Reno's National Automobile Museum for its 1999 display. For the first 10 years of its life, the wagon was used as a "summer" car on a Maine estate.

The station wagon body on this circa-1939 Mack ED was probably made by Cantrell. *Mack*

Here we see the 1939 Plymouth's rear doors open.

This maroon 1939 Plymouth wagon was photographed at Wavecrest 1999.

Tom Williams owns this maroon 1939 Pontiac.

Williams' 1939 Pontiac has a split back bumper.

This lowered 1939 Pontiac was photographed at
Wavecrest 1999.

Arlen Roth, of New York, bought this 1940 Buick wagon in 1988. It was initially sold in Wisconsin. Roth has done limited work on the vehicle. *Arlen Roth*

This 1940 Buick was photographed at Wavecrest 1999. Note the fog lights. The vehicle is painted maroon. In 1940, Buick began selling production station wagons.

The 1940 Buick wagon's maroon paint is original. Note the old Buick dealership sign. *Arlen Roth*

The taillight of the Roth Buick is at the top, and the light saying "BUICK EIGHT" also functions as a turn indicator and is attached to the door for the spare-tire compartment. According to Roth, when the wagons first came out, the spare tire would not fit through the opening, and Buick sent out a service bulletin telling dealers to shave away enough wood to allow the tire to pass through. *Arlen Roth*

This close-up of the Roth Buick shows that the wood has aged nicely and now shows some of the character associated with its long service. *Arlen Roth*

Don Fistler, of Illinois, owns this restored 1940 Chevrolet Special DeLuxe station wagon. *Don Fistler*

This close-up shows the paneling in the door of Fistler's Chevrolet. *Don Fistler*

On Fistler's Chevrolet, the body
is black and the wheels are red.
Its rear bumper is split, and the
top is covered with fabric.
Don Fistler

Fistler's tailgate is down to
display some of his Green Bay
Packers memorabilia.
Don Fistler

A circa-1940 Crosley is shown entering the gates of Fort Sheridan, Illinois. According to the 1942 Signal Corps caption, the MP said "No roller skating allowed on the main thoroughfare" to the two ladies in the station wagon, who were Army hostesses. The Fort Sheridan MPs called this vehicle a "Bug." Crosleys were built until 1952. *Fred Crismon*

This circa-1940 Dodge light-truck chassis was fitted with a station wagon body and used by the military. *Fred Crismon*

THE 1940 FORD V-8 STATION WAGONS

THE STYLING of the De Luxe Ford Station Wagon makes it definitely at home on the finest estate. As a passenger vehicle, it seats eight—including driver—and it is quickly converted into a utility hauling unit by removing rear and center seats. It's roomier inside for 1940, and seats have been redesigned and respaced to take advantage of the extra inches. It has the new, convenient Finger-Tip Gearshift on the steering post. Front seat is adjustable. Windshield and windows are Safety Glass. Doors and tail gate can be locked. Spare wheel is mounted on the tail gate. 85 hp Ford V-8 performance—big hydraulic brakes—Ford reliability, economy and long life.

* The lower priced Ford V-8 Station Wagon has the modern front end styling of the Ford V-8 passenger car. It has the same big, powerful hydraulic brakes, the same kind of quality in the chassis construction, the same 8-cylinder performance, the same seating

Ford's station wagon offerings for 1940 are shown in this excerpt from the 1940 company's commercial car and truck literature. The DeLuxe 1940 model is the larger one. The standard one is shown at the lower left and was similar in appearance to the 1939 DeLuxe model, a practice that Ford followed in the late 1930s of making the previous year's DeLuxe model similar to this year's standard.

David Merritt, of Arizona, owns this restored 1940 Ford wagon. *David Merritt*

A view inside the front right door of Merritt's Ford shows the restored interior. *David Merritt*

This interior shot of the Luchsinger Ford shows the wooden paneling on the door's inside.

Dave and Cheryl Luchsinger's 1940 Ford was photographed on the pier at Santa Cruz.

Jim Fergus owns this 1940 Ford DeLuxe. It has been repowered with a Chevrolet engine.

The body on Fergus' Ford looks original.

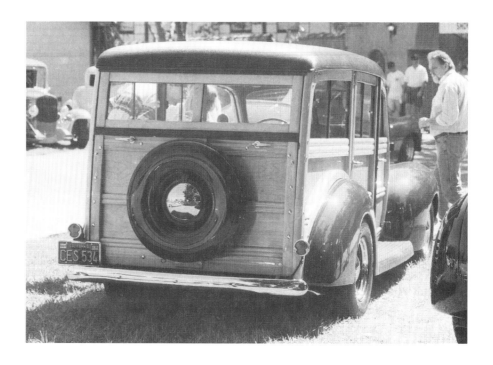

This 1940 Ford DeLuxe was lowered and received the flame treatment. The flames are orange and blue.

Dallas and Willa Paul own this 1940 Ford DeLuxe, which has been both lowered and repowered.

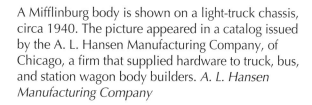

Suburban station wagon built by Mifflinburg Body Co. Space in rear for luggage. Side doors fitted with Hansen Cab Lock permit easy entrance and exit. Aisle between front seats. Luggage is loaded into space behind rear seat and kept in place by end gate. The end gate is fitted with Hansen End Gate Lock, which slams shut and is operated by outside handle.

A Mifflinburg body is shown on a light-truck chassis, circa 1940. The picture appeared in a catalog issued by the A. L. Hansen Manufacturing Company, of Chicago, a firm that supplied hardware to truck, bus, and station wagon body builders. *A. L. Hansen Manufacturing Company*

This life-sized cutout of a 1940 Ford wagon graces the front of a restaurant near Key Largo, Florida.

This 1940 Oldsmobile was photographed at Wavecrest 1999. It's painted tannish gray.

This is the Hansen end gate lock, used on the Mifflinburg station wagon body. The picture appeared in the Hansen catalog. *A. L. Hansen Manufacturing Company*

HANSEN END GATE LOCK

THE Hansen End Gate Lock is specially designed for end gates. It can be applied to gates of any width merely by cutting off rods to desired length. Where there is a three-quarter rear door and end gate, this lock may be used. Also in numerous other ways, such as tire compartment boxes, etc.

A few of the types of bodies to which the No. 98 End Gate Lock is adaptable include—panel—open express—canopy top express—screen side express—pickup body—station wagon or suburban body.

NO. 98 END GATE LOCK, showing reversed type striker bolt cases and method of applying lock to gate. Striker bolt slide, rod and center mechanism fit into the mortised space. Standard rod, 26" long. Moving parts cadmium plated, including rods, center mechanism and striker bolts. Lead-coated striker bolt cases and center case. Weight, 2 lbs.

Ralph Wilson and Matilda Dodge Wilson (the automotive heiress) had the Meteor Motor Car Company outfit this 1940 LaSalle with an extended chassis. The current owner is Jim Fleischer, who loaned it to the Petersen Automotive Museum. The museum's description said, in part, that the Wilsons used the vehicle on their Meadow Brook estate to "transport servants into Detroit on their days off and to drive the local school football team to and from games. Since the LaSalle could carry the same number of passengers as two standard-size cars, it was considered economical since the original owners did not have to purchase a second vehicle or go to the expense of hiring an additional driver." LaSalle production ended in 1940.

This 1940 International with a wooden station wagon body was photographed at Wavecrest 1999.

This rear view of the 1940 International shows its tailgate down and the rear of the third seat.

The original buyer of this 1940 Packard needed a larger body than was available with Packard's standard station wagon, so the custom body was built by the New England Auto Body Works of New Haven, Connecticut. Note that the door handles point down. Arlen Roth is its third owner. *Arlen Roth*

The Packard's owners have kept nearly all records of the vehicle's repairs and maintenance. The suspension had to be strengthened to hold the body's greater weight. *Arlen Roth*

The ceiling of the 1940 Packard features this neat dome light. *Arlen Roth*

On each side of the 1940 Packard's rear license plate is a tool drawer. *Arlen Roth*

This 1940 Plymouth, in the midst of undergoing a thorough restoration, visited Wavecrest 1999.

Rear and side rear doors
have yet to be fitted on
the 1940 Plymouth.
Note the wooden roofing.

Here's an attractive gray 1940 Pontiac station wagon seen at Wavecrest 1999.

This picture of a 1940 Willys station wagon appeared in a magazine ad. That year Willys offered a three-year/100,000-mile guarantee.

CHAPTER 4

1941–1950

The 1941 model year was probably the best year up to that time, in terms of woody sales. Most automakers were offering a station wagon line and some even offered station wagons at different levels of trim (for example, standard and deluxe). Reworking some figures given by Ron Kowalke, here are estimates of 1941 station wagon production: Buick 838; Chevrolet 4,790; Chrysler 1,000; Crosley 150; Ford 16,766; Hudson 179; Mercury 2,080; Oldsmobile 699; Packard 600; Plymouth 2,700; Pontiac 1,714; and Willys 400.

This decade was split by World War II, and production of 1942 autos was limited because the United States entered the war shortly after production of 1942 models began. Nevertheless, many of those autos built exhibited new styling: many wagon bodies had been redesigned to be lower than in earlier years, and this was caused by the general trends in streamlining. From the standpoint of woody styling, Chrysler should get high marks. Its 1941–1942 Town & Country models were beautiful, and they demonstrated an effort at streamlining the rear of the station wagon.

Because of the war, surviving 1942 station wagons are relatively rare. Many of the 1942 wagons were drafted into military service and painted either olive drab or battleship gray. Production facilities were

Gillig Corporation has been located in the San Francisco Bay Area for many years. The company was first known for producing roofs to enclose open auto bodies. It built many truck and bus bodies, and in recent years, the company has been known for its buses. Here is a 1941 Cadillac chassis that Gillig outfitted with a station wagon body. When viewing the Cadillac from the rear, it appears that the spare-tire compartment is below the third seat. The license bracket is on the left. There appear to be shades on the two side rear doors. *Gillig Corporation*

This well-preserved 1941 Chevrolet wagon was photographed at a Santa Cruz meet.

The metalwork on the 1941 Chevrolet is painted navy blue. Note the split rear bumper, to accommodate the spare.

converted to producing war materiel, and Ford's station wagon body works began producing wooden gliders.

During the war, many station wagons were enlarged to minibus proportions so they could carry more war workers. A person working for Hercules-Campbell explained: "After the war started we received 200 new Chevrolet two- and four-passenger cars, which we were to cut off the bodies from and install station wagon bodies which could carry eight passengers." Wood and other nonmetals were often the materials used in such undertakings. The Cantrell history said that due to a shortage of autos during the war, "this often meant converting sedans into station wagons. The car would be cut in two, the frame and driveshaft extended, and wood built into the sectioned area." Marmon-Herrington had produced four-wheel-drive conversions for Ford chassis since the mid-1930s. Some Ford station wagons used during World War II had that four-wheel-drive feature.

Michael Lamm wrote that "After World War II, station wagons became increasingly popular as family transportation. The station wagon body style moved from the landed gentry, the film industry and the

Charles and Mary Jane Mitchell own this 1941 Chrysler, which is shown "passing in review" at the 1997 Greenwich Concours in Connecticut. *Gregg D. Merksamer*

ranch to the suburbs. It was now the vehicle in which mom took the kids to school, the dog to the vet and dad to the train station."

Postwar tastes may have shifted to station wagons, but not back to the prewar style of the station wagon. Writing in *Automobile Quarterly*, Dave Emanuel said that the prewar types of station wagons "wouldn't do. While they were aesthetically pleasing, wood bodies were simply too expensive to build and maintain; keeping the wood in good shape meant revarnishing every two to three years, and the body-attaching bolts required constant attention. Such chores made station wagon ownership an albatross that would never be worn by the mainstream of the car-buying public."

American vehicles offered through about 1948 were warmed-over 1942 models. In 1949, auto builders introduced new models with major restyling, and nearly every one offered a station wagon with real wood trim as a styling flare.

For many automakers, this would be the last style of wooden wagons they built.

Once again, Ford led the woody pack by using a metal frame in 1949. Lorin Sorensen wrote this about the 1949 Ford (and Mercury) station wagon bodies: "Instead of the traditional wood frame box, the bodies

This side view of the Mitchell Chrysler shows humpback body lines that are somewhere between those of a sedan and a more typical wagon. The longer roof was also used on Chrysler's limousine. *Gregg D. Merksamer*

Peter Heydon, of Michigan, owns this 1941 Chrysler wagon. It was originally owned by Warner Brothers Studios and appeared in some *Our Gang* and *Charlie Chan* movies. *Peter N. Heydon*

This close-up of Heydon's wagon shows the distinctive lines of the trunk. *Peter N. Heydon*

were now all-steel with the hardwood and plywood panels bolted on strictly for effect. The idea was to maintain the rugged good looks and tradition of the wood cars and yet eliminate the customary squeaks and groans by transferring body stresses to the newly engineered two-door steel body shell."

By 1950, a number of automakers would be offering all-steel station wagon bodies, and the buyer could choose between them, wooden bodies, and metal bodies trimmed with wood.

Nevertheless, wooden station wagon bodies remained available from outside builders for several types of light trucks. They offered several advantages over wagons built on auto chassis: they had more headroom, their cargo-carrying capacity was greater, they had higher ground clearance, and they were better suited to operation over rough terrain. I am very partial to trucks, and this book pays relatively more attention to truck-based station wagons than do most books on woodys.

As mentioned earlier, station wagons increased greatly in popularity after the war. Steve Manning estimated that in 1940, station wagons accounted for less than 1 percent of new cars sold. By 1950, this figure had increased to about 3 percent.

Looking at the National Woody Club roster for the 1941–1950 decade, we see the following for makes with totals greater than four: 63 Buicks, 115 Chevrolets, 134 Chryslers, 9 DeSotos, 32 Dodges, 783 Fords, 160 Mercurys, 37 Oldsmobiles, 34 Packards, 89 Plymouths, and 58 Pontiacs. Again, Fords predominate: there were 178 from 1947 and 160 from 1946.

This is a view inside the trunk of a 1941 Chrysler Town & Country. The doors open to each side, in "clamshell" fashion. This photo was taken at the Silverado Concours, about 1980. The emblem below the window says "Chrysler fluid drive." Fluid drive was a semiautomatic transmission available on some Chrysler Corporation autos.

This 1941 Ford wagon is owned by Walt Nakamura.

Nakamura's Ford looks to be in good shape.

Mercer County, New Jersey, used what is probably a 1941 Ford station wagon for its bookmobile. *American Library Association*

The Canadian Army used this 1941 Ford station wagon with oversized tires. The photo was taken in England in 1944. *Public Archives of Canada*

Here's a family of Ford trucks in 1941: a station wagon, a bus, and a COE semi-tractor that pulls a horse trailer. "Joy Farms" is painted on the wagon and the bus. *Lorin Sorensen*

The U.S. Navy used this 1941 International station wagon, seen passing a guard gate. *Fred Crismon*

After studying pictures of so many fine-looking station wagons, it's hard to find a favorite. In this instance, I will play favorites and say that if I were to win the California lottery, this is the year and make of station wagon I'd like to own: a 1942 Chrysler.

This 1942 Chrysler was photographed at Wavecrest 1999. Note how the chrome stripe pattern from the front (see previous photo) carries over to the rear fenders.

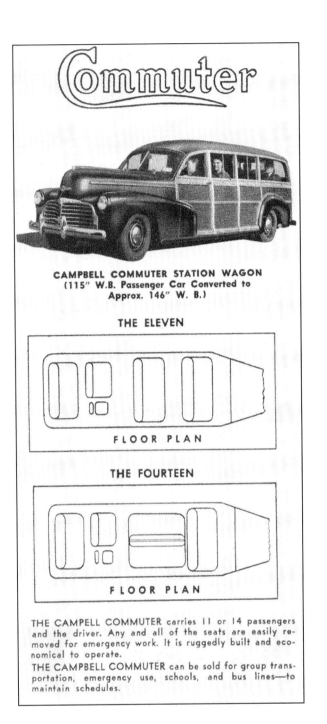

Commuter

CAMPBELL COMMUTER STATION WAGON
(115" W.B. Passenger Car Converted to
Approx. 146" W. B.)

THE ELEVEN

FLOOR PLAN

THE FOURTEEN

FLOOR PLAN

THE CAMPELL COMMUTER carries 11 or 14 passengers
and the driver. Any and all of the seats are easily removed for emergency work. It is ruggedly built and economical to operate.
THE CAMPBELL COMMUTER can be sold for group transportation, emergency use, schools, and bus lines—to
maintain schedules.

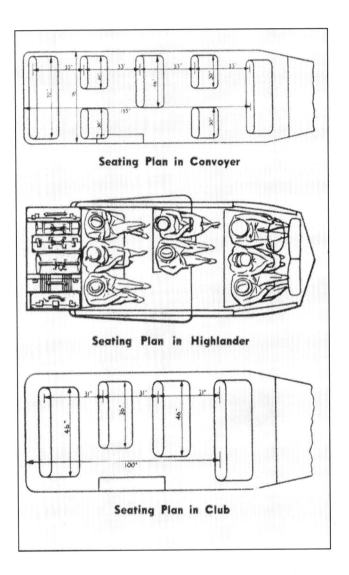

Seating Plan in Convoyer

Seating Plan in Highlander

Seating Plan in Club

Campbell offered this body for 1942–1947 Chevrolet
auto chassis that were extended to 146 inches. It
could carry up to 14 passengers with one seating
configuration having some seats mounted back-to-
back, and facing to either side of the vehicle.

Seating arrangements for three Campbell Chevrolet
light-truck station wagon bodies are shown here.

For 125 ¼ " W.B.
Chassis

The CLUB

The Campbell Club Station Wagon accommodates 11 passengers and driver and is expressly designed for schools, country clubs, hotels, camps, plants, depots, etc. The unit contains full width driver's seat, 2 intermediate seats and a full width rear seat, which are easily removable.

The HIGHLANDER

The Campbell Highlander accommodates 6-8 passengers and driver and is expressly designed for depots, camps, etc., requiring extra load ability. The unit contains full width driver's seat, one ¾ intermediate seat and a full width rear seat.

For 116" W.B. Chassis

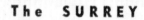

The SURREY

The Campbell Surrey Station Wagon has the same seating capacity as the club body. It is longer, resulting in greater seat spacing and more load carrying ability.

For 137" W.B. Chassis

MID-STATE BODY COMPANY, Inc.
WATERLOO, NEW YORK

These Campbell bodies were for mounting on 1942–1947 Chevrolet light-truck chassis with wheelbases of 116, 125, and 137 inches. An even larger model, the Campbell "Convoyer," was intended for the 161-inch chassis, and could carry up to 18 passengers. The 1942 Chevrolet pictured at the top has Red Cross markings.

This nicely preserved 1942 Ford station wagon was photographed at Wavecrest 1999. Its color is light aqua.

The Schnabel Company was a well-known Pennsylvania truck and trailer body builder. Schnabel's plaque stands in front of this picture of a 1942 Chrysler Town & Country pulling a matching dog trailer. It's likely that Schnabel built the trailer. *Historical Society of Western Pennsylvania*

Surfboard equipped and ready for the beach, a whole row of late 1940s Ford wagons were lined up at the Santa Cruz pier in 1999.

This close-up of a 1947 Ford Sportsman shows the door and rear panels.

Above: For a southern California flavor, Erickson's wagon carries California plates, a UCLA decal, and blue-beaded taillight lenses.

Left: Tom Erickson, of British Columbia, owns this lowered maroon 1947 Ford wagon.

Above: Rich and Barb Bloedl own this customized 1947 wagon. It has been lowered and is painted cherry red.

Above: On this highly customized Ford, from either 1947 or 1948, the hood, windshield frame, and grille are painted flat orange; its fenders are flat black.

The customized Ford's top has been cut off, but the remaining wood appears to be original. The photos were taken in Santa Cruz.

J. W. Silvera
owns this dark
gray 1947
Mercury wagon,
which was
photographed at
Santa Cruz.

Above: The roofline of the 1947 Nash
suburban sedan slopes downward in the
rear, rather than having the boxy shape and
extra room of a conventional station wagon
body. *Betty and Jim Fritts*

Left: Here's a close-up shot of the right rear
of the Fritts' Nash. *Betty and Jim Fritts*

In the postwar years, Nash sold a "suburban" model, which was their four-door sedan trimmed with wood. This 1947 model belongs to Betty and Jim Fritts, of Florida, who bought it in 1992 and have subsequently restored it. The car is completely stock, and is painted blue. Nash autos became Ramblers in 1957. *Betty and Jim Fritts*

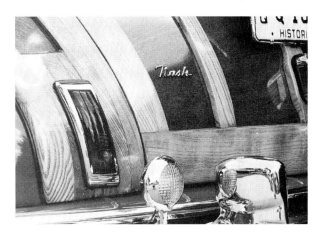

This detail shot taken of the 1947 Nash's left rear corner shows several lights. *Betty and Jim Fritts*

On this 1947 Nash, the trunk area is paneled with wood, and the spare tire rides flat. The rear seat folds flat and converts into a bed. *Betty and Jim Fritts*

In this advertising postcard, a postwar Olds station wagon was parked at the side of a New Jersey restaurant. The wagon's metalwork was painted the same shade of blue as the restaurant's trim.

This is a one-of-a-kind motor home built on a new 1947 Packard limousine (148-inch-wheelbase) chassis. The original builder was Howard Dawes, president of the Howard All-Steel Trailer Company, of Saginaw, Michigan, and it was the prototype of a self-powered camper. *Charles M. Collins*

The Packard-based motor home was sold to Jim Miller and then named the *Mil-Col Land Yacht*, as we can see here.
Charles M. Collins

The *Land Yacht's* body is aluminum and the roof bows are of steel. The roof is of pine, shaped in boat-hull fashion, and secured by brass screws. The roof covering is aircraft fabric.
Charles M. Collins

Far left: Looking at the front corner of the *Land Yacht*, we see the wood used in the roof and a turn indicator.
Charles M. Collins

Left: The *Land Yacht's* grille is made of oak, which helps qualify this rig as a "woody."
Charles M. Collin

With surfboards on top and in need of work along its sides, this 1947 Plymouth was on display at Wavecrest 1999.

Raymond G. Tomasello owns this 1948 Buick Super Estate Wagon with a Hercules body, which was on display at the National Automobile Museum in Reno. With some minor exceptions, the vehicle is in its original condition.

This 1948 Chevrolet wagon with a Hawaiian theme appeared in the year 2000 Fourth of July parade in Larkspur, California.

The 1948 Chevrolet wagon sags in the rear because of its load of passengers riding on the tailgate.

CHEVROLET-CANTRELL STATION WAGONS

1947 CANTRELL STATION WAGON BODY SPECIFICATIONS FOR THE NEW HALF TON CHEVROLET TRUCK CHASSIS

General Construction: Ash frame structure with mahogany or red gum panels. All outside joints glued with water-proof and fungus-proof glue. All component parts submerged in wood preservative for three minutes before assembly as a precaution against dry rot, fungus and insect attack. Finished with best quality varnish. Complete safety glass enclosure. Glass operated by regulators on front doors; sliding glass in all other side windows. Lift door above tailgate in rear full width of body, supported by a continuous leak-proof hinge along top edge. The tailgate has a continuous hinge along lower edge and is supported by covered chains when lowered to the horizontal position.

Seats: Seat cushions and back cushions are constructed with soft, deep inner-coil springs and covered with brown artificial leather. Three seats are provided with a capacity for eight people. The middle seat may be removed and the rear seat moved forward or both seats may be removed for additional luggage space. No tools are needed to remove these seats.

Floor covering: The driver's compartment provided with Chevrolet floor mat; rear compartment covered with heavy ribbed rubber matting, or equal.

Locks: Provision is made for completely locking car doors, windows, tailgate, and lift door.

Tail-Light and License Plate Bracket: Mounted high in the middle of tailgate, using our swinging bracket to permit vertical position when driving with tailgate in lowered position.

Spare Wheel: The spare wheel is mounted under the rear end of the chassis.

Bumpers: Full length bumpers, front and rear, are provided with chassis.

J. T. CANTRELL and CO. • Huntington Station, New York

The J. T. Cantrell & Company advertised this station wagon body for the 1948 Chevrolet light-truck chassis. Extra chrome strips on the fenders were an option for Chevrolet trucks.

The trunk on this 1948 Chrysler Town & Country is metal, painted a brownish rust color. Strips of wood are added along the edges, forming a cross in the trunk's center. The photo was taken at an auction site in Scottsdale in early 2001.

Bob Breisford owns this 1948 Chrysler Town & Country. It's painted maroon.

Shown is a rear view of Breisford's 1948 Chrysler, taken on the Santa Cruz pier in 1999.

Jim and Kathy Bringhurst own this 1948 Ford. The Bringhursts loaned it to the National Automobile Museum in Reno for its "Woody World" display. The structural wood is original, although the panels are new. The vehicle is now powered by a 406-ci Chevrolet engine, and it has air conditioning.

This 1948 GMC has a Campbell Highlander body, and belongs to Don and Emma Gilbert, of Arizona, who restored it. Their work included replacing all 17 pieces of glass, disassembling the front-end sheet metal, repainting the interior, refacing and rebuilding the gauges, reupholstering the interior, rebuilding the engine, replacing all rubber seals, and replating the chrome. The Gilberts use the wagon to promote their own old-truck-parts business. *Don and Emma Gilbert*

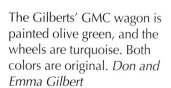

Above: Here's the Campbell-built nameplate of the Gilberts' GMC, with a body, or job, number stamped at the top. *Don and Emma Gilbert*

Right: A previous owner had replaced some wood and refinished the wooden body on the Gilberts' GMC. *Don and Emma Gilbert*

The Gilberts' GMC wagon is painted olive green, and the wheels are turquoise. Both colors are original. *Don and Emma Gilbert*

Pictured here are child-sized station wagons in front of a 1948 Mercury.

The back of the 1948 Olds is loaded with picnic gear (rather than surfboards).

Shown is a maroon 1948 Oldsmobile photographed at Wavecrest 1999.

This 1946–1948 Plymouth has fog lights. The picture was taken in 1999 at Wavecrest.

Above: This maroon 1948 Pontiac wagon was seen at the 1999 Kruse auction in Scottsdale, Arizona. It needs some work (and some door handles).

James Bruno owns this 1948 Pontiac. The surfboard on top was autographed by one of the Beach Boys. The photo was taken at the Greenwich Concours in 1999. *Gregg D. Merksamer*

At Wavecrest 1999 the display area overflowed, and some station wagons had to park on the beach. Here, we see a 1948 Pontiac on the beach.

Pat and Mary Brooks
own this 1949
Buick wagon. It
participated in the
1997 Peking-to-Paris
Motor Challenge.
Gregg D. Merksamer

The Brooks' 1949
Buick is outside New
York's Palace Hotel.
Gregg D. Merksamer

Andy Berenson owns this 1949 Bentley Mark VI Continental Tourer. The frame is oak, and the panels are mahogany. *Gregg D. Merksamer*

The Bentley's rear door opens to the side. These photos were taken at the Greenwich, Connecticut, Concours in 2000. *Gregg D. Merksamer*

Bill and Cindy Halliday loaned this 1949 Chevrolet to the National Automobile Museum for its "Woody World" display in Reno in 1999 and 2000. In 1949 the wagon was sold new in Hemet, California, and during the 1960s it served as a surfer's wagon.

The 1949 Chevrolet's metal is painted maroon. Note the piano hinge along the bottom of the tailgate.

Highway-department employees are shown surveying road users. At left is a circa-1949 Chevrolet light-truck chassis with a wooden body. One of the survey crew sits on its ample fenders. *San Mateo Historical Museum*

This 1949 Chrysler convertible with Town & Country trim was photographed at Wavecrest 1999.

The 1949 Chrysler convertible is painted bright red. Note that the paneling is metal; only the trim is wood.

Dorna and Rowland Baker own this 1949 Dodge station wagon.

Mike Lady owns this 1949 Chrysler Town & Country. Note the rear-mounted spare.

Note the split rear bumper of the Bakers' 1949 Dodge.

This 1949 Mercury, spotted on the Santa Cruz pier, needs major work.

This 1949 Dodge has a Cantrell body, and it belongs to C. Carter Walker Jr., of Connecticut. Walker bought the wagon in 1970 and began its restoration about 10 years later. *C. Carter Walker Jr.*

Note the fine detail as we look at the roof above the rear window on Walker's Dodge. Its rear seat is not original; the seat was built by a cabinet-builder friend of Walker's. The floral pillow is also not original equipment. *C. Carter Walker Jr.*

The 1949 Dodge body's cargo-carrying capacity is large. The front and rear bumpers are painted black, but the body is painted blue-green. *C. Carter Walker Jr.*

The Adena, Ohio, volunteer fire department used this 1949 Dodge wagon as an ambulance and to transport personnel.

The 1949 Dodge was photographed at an auction in Scottsdale, Arizona, in early 2001.

Ron and Karen Wright own this highly customized 1949 Ford. Its license plates read, "WUDWGN."

This maroon 1949 Packard station wagon was photographed at Wavecrest 1999.

Nick Alexander owns this gray 1949 Mercury wagon.

Alexander's 1949 Mercury was photographed on the pier at Santa Cruz.

Another 1949 Packard, this one photographed at Santa Cruz. Packard autos were built until the late 1950s.

Note how the curvature of the body line is continued in the woodwork on this 1949 Packard.

This photo was taken at the 1985 Krause Car Show and shows a 1949 Plymouth station wagon in need of headlight rims. *Ray Scroggins*

This cream-colored 1949 Plymouth with fog lights, roof rack, and visor was photographed at Santa Cruz in 1999. In 1949, Plymouth also sold an all-metal two-door wagon.

Ray Unsworth, of Vermont, owns this maroon 1949 Plymouth wagon. The rear bumperettes fold down so the tailgate can lie flat. *Ray Unsworth*

This maroon 1949 Pontiac is shown on the pier at Santa Cruz in 1999.

Sitting on the Roth Buick's tailgate is a late 1930s Garton woody pedal car. *Arlen Roth*

Arlen Roth, of New York, bought this 1950 Buick in 1996. It has been completely restored. *Arlen Roth*

This 1950 Buick is in need of restoration. Someday it will look like the Buick wagon shown to the left.

Much of the wood on this 1950 Buick will have to be replaced.

The library system in upstate New York used this circa-1950 Chevrolet light truck with a station wagon body for delivering books to branch libraries. *American Library Association*

This shiny 1950 Chrysler convertible was photographed at Wavecrest 1999.

A "Town & Country " badge is mounted to the lower right of this 1950 Chrysler's trunk lid. The taillights are on the outer edge of the fender.

A surf shop in Laguna Beach, California, uses this 1950 Ford station wagon for promotional purposes.

A surfboard sticks out from the rear of the custom Ford. The rig is painted an orange red, and the woodwork is not in its original colors.

The Texas license plates on this 1950
Ford proclaim, "WOOD IS GOOD."

This black 1950 Ford wagon looks
original. It carries a "for sale" sign
in the front window.

This tan 1950
Ford wagon was
photographed in
front of an art
display at a
California station
wagon meet.
Note the graphic
of a surfer riding
the waves just
above the
"custom" emblem.

Bob Theda owns this 1950 Ford. The body and chrome have been painted a metallic gray green.

This side view of Theda's 1950 Ford shows that it was both chopped and lowered.

This 1950 Plymouth, photographed at Wavecrest 1999, was undergoing major metal and wood repairs.

The 1950 Plymouth's fenders and rear door were all of different colors, so some must be off of a parts wagon. Surfboards are on the roof; the owner has at least two ways to spend his weekends.

Ernest C. Fodor owns this 1950 Plymouth, which was photographed in Bethlehem, Pennsylvania, in 1998. It looks to be in showroom condition. *Gregg D. Merksamer*

Steve Howard, of Washington State, owns this 1950 Studebaker Champion. Initially, it was a four-door sedan. Howard custom-built the body from the firewall back, which took six years. The vehicle is now powered by a Chevrolet 350-ci engine. *Steve Howard*

Above: Howard used hard rock maple and birch paneling. The rear bumper is made of wood; there is no front bumper. The wagon is painted emerald green. *Steve Howard*

Right: Note the detail in the ceiling of Howard's Studebaker. The seats are from an Oldsmobile van. Studebakers were built until the mid-1960s. *Steve Howard*

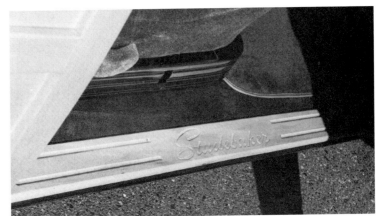

The Studebaker logo is hand-carved in the door sills of Howard's car. *Steve Howard*

CHAPTER 5

1951-1960

The true woodys died sometime in the early 1950s. For each make the date of death differed. Donald J. Narus, in his encyclopedic *Great American Woodies & Wagons*, said this of the year 1954: "Buick introduced an all-steel wagon this year. From now on any and all Woodies produced were special order cars, or of limited production. Cantrell still made such Woodys on truck chassis for Chevrolet, GMC, Dodge and Studebaker. New for this year was the Buick Century Estate Wagon and the Special Estate Wagon. Neither had a hint of wood, even simulated wood."

Woodys waned in popularity because the wooden bodies had become too expensive to build and too difficult to maintain. Also, woodys were seen as less safe than steel cars because, as Ken Gross wrote, "In a collision, wood bodies virtually exploded and (if you survived), you'd end up with a pile of matchsticks."

Though wood was rapidly replaced by steel in the 1950s, the actual station wagon body style remained

Ray Unsworth owns this 1951 Buick Roadmaster wagon. *Ray Unsworth*

Unsworth's Buick is shown with its tailgate down. *Ray Unsworth*

popular, covered with simulated wood trim, and then plain metal. The only other styling comment to be made is that as the auto bodies were made lower, the station wagon bodies built on the same lines had lower interiors. This reduced cargo-carrying space and made access to the seat in the far rear more difficult. An improvement for many auto-based wagons was the introduction of fold-down rear seats, which were easier to deal with than having to physically remove the wagon's rear seats in order to load freight.

The few remaining wagon bodies built on light-truck chassis offered higher interior heights and higher road clearance than did station wagon bodies offered on passenger-car chassis.

The 1954 edition of *The Silver Book* contained only one page showing Campbell bodies, apparently made of wood. There were advertisements from several builders of all-steel station wagons, often marketed as small school buses. Some builders also offered "stretch" versions of conventional four-door sedans.

A few "custom" wooden wagons continued to be built on passenger-car chassis. Also, wood trim was used in a handful of "show" cars that auto manufacturers used for display at auto shows. Some of these have fallen into the hands of collectors.

By the end of the 1950s, the wooden "woody" had disappeared, replaced by all-steel bodies, sometimes with fake wooden finishes. For this decade, the National Woody Club's roster tapers off, reflecting the end of wooden bodies. For makes with totals greater than four we see the following: 56 Buicks, 20 Chevrolets, 155 Fords, and 26 Mercurys. For this decade, as well as all others, Fords predominate.

John Winter, of Arizona, owns this 1951 Dodge. It has a Cantrell body and has been completely restored. Winter installed a four-speed gearbox and a regular clutch to replace the wagon's original fluid drive, which made the wagon too sluggish to operate in today's traffic. *John Winter*

This is the interior panel of the left rear door of Winter's Dodge. *John Winter*

Shown are details in the Dodge's overhead woodwork. *John Winter*

This view shows the roof woodwork looking toward the rear. *John Winter*

Shown is the top tailgate latch mechanism of Winter's Dodge. *John Winter*

James Goren owns this 1951 Fiat Giardinetta Legno station wagon. It was photographed at the Concours held in Greenwich, Connecticut, in 2000. Barely visible is the sunroof, which is covered with canvas. *Gregg D. Merksamer*

The Fiat's engine originally produced 18 horsepower, but this was boosted to an impressive 23 by adding twin carbs and replacing the thermo-siphon cooling with a water pump. *Gregg D. Merksamer*

This is a 1985 photo taken at the Iola, Wisconsin, car show, and it shows a 1951 Ford Country Squire owned by Jim Rodell. *Ray Scroggins*

David Doyle owned this 1951 Ford Country Squire, painted light blue. It has an exterior sun visor, a popular accessory at that time. The photo was taken at Iola in 1985. *Ray Scroggins*

Linda Kirsten, of Washington State, owns this nicely preserved 1951 Ford wagon.

Kirsten's Ford wagon is aqua in color.

This trailered 1951 Ford wagon was photographed at Santa Cruz. Its side panels are being restored, and it looks like the front is being customized.

Arlen Roth, of New York, owns this 1951 Mercury. It has been modified to enhance its performance. *Arlen Roth*

This view is from the right rear of Roth's Mercury. Note the spare-tire cover. *Arlen Roth*

Wood continued to be used for framing some truck bodies until well into the decade. This is a Gerstenslager moving-van body, built on an early-1950s White chassis. We see a front corner of the cab to the right plus the framing for the body above the cab and to the rear. *Gerstenslager Corporation*

This is the completed Gerstenslager moving-van body. *Gerstenslager Corporation*

This 1952 Mercury station wagon was photographed in Santa Cruz, California.

The exterior of this 1952 Chevrolet wagon is metal, but its interior paneling is wood. The Oregon plates say "52 WOOD."

Mike McKay owns this customized 1952 Chevrolet wagon. The lights or reflectors just above the rear bumper have been added.

G. C. Larson owns
this maroon 1953
Buick Super
station wagon.
Ray Scroggins

This rear view of Larson's 1953 Buick shows extensive use of wood in the tailgate; 1953 would be the last year for
Buick woody wagons. *Ray Scroggins*

This 1953 Buick wagon was photographed at Wavecrest 1999.

In the early 1950s, Chevrolet went from using wood to metal with a woodgrain pattern. This 1953 Chevrolet wagon was "stretched" by the Armbruster Company of Fort Smith, Arkansas, so that it could carry up to 15 passengers.

This circa-1953 International carried a homemade wooden camping box. *State of West Virginia*

This advertisement shows Campbell chassis for placement on Chevrolet light-truck chassis. Four sizes were offered, and each fit on a different wheelbase. The largest could accommodate 18 passengers.

This is a full-sized all-wood replica of a 1957 GMC pickup, located in the Hays Antique Truck Museum.

Bernard Glieberman owns this 1955 Lincoln Sportsman, which was on display at the Petersen Automotive Museum in Los Angeles. It was one of 12 "colour" cars built by Lincoln for display at auto shows throughout the United States. It's based on a Lincoln Capri convertible body but paneled in Honduras teak and framed with genuine maple. The steering wheel, gearshift knob, and turn indicator handle are all made of wood.

Bob Taylor
owns this well-
cared-for 1958
Morris Minor,
which was
photographed
on the Santa
Cruz pier.

Note the split
rear bumper
of the 1958
Morris Minor.

Len Billingsley, of California, owns this British-built 1959 Morris. Billingsley found it in 1978, in badly rusted condition and lacking a motor and transmission.

This view of the rear shows the wood, some of which is original, on Billingsley's Morris. The metal is painted a 1990 Chevrolet color, dark beachwood brown. It was photographed in Auburn, California.

Billingsley's wagon was on display at the National Automobile Museum's "Woody World" exhibition, where this photo was taken.

Wicker is a form of wood, and this 1960 Fiat has wicker seats that can be removed, say, when one is at the beach.

Stan Reichl used
the chassis of a
1960 Chevrolet
to carry this
wooden body.
*Liz and Stan
Reichl*

The rig is used to advertise Reichl's radiator business. *Liz and Stan Reichl*

CHAPTER 6

1961 to The Present

Many aging woodys got a chance at a second childhood when they were acquired by surfers, who liked to carry their boards in the long, spacious rear compartments. The old woodys became a status symbol for the surfing set in the 1960s. Auto customizers also liked old woodys because the wood was easier to work with than metal. Restorers liked them, too, because they felt as if they could do a larger share of a woody's restoration since they could handle the wood part. As David Miller (who bought a 1940 GMC woody in dire need of restoration) explained: "If it had wheels, I liked it. If it was wood, I could work it." More recently, considerable collector interest has developed in preserving woodys in their original state. A number of small firms specialize in woody restoration.

Woodys remain very collectable and their prices are climbing, if not soaring. An article in the Petersen Automotive Museum's newsletter contained an interview with George Coleman, who handles numerous woody sales transactions and gives insight on the woody market: "Who buys woodys? Coleman's customers are 'laid-back' personalities, deliberate, conservative people who appreciate the good things in life. His woodys appeal to real estate agents and to owners of bed-and-breakfasts and hunting lodges. Surprisingly, 40 percent of his customers are female."

According to Coleman, the popularity trend line is shifting to newer woodys as our population ages. Ford Model A wagons were once popular but, he explains, "they're pretty cold now. Any car that's 1935 or down,

Here's a 1962 Chevrolet pickup with a rustic wooden camping or live-in body, photographed in San Francisco.

is hard to sell. Each year or so that moves up a notch." Sales of Ford wagons built from 1949 to 1951 are climbing. According to Coleman, "They'll get hotter because they drive better, and most people relate to them." (Coleman's favorite wagons are prewar Packards, although he thinks that they do not drive as well as later cars.)

Many of the custom woodys we see today are the result of the individual efforts of people skilled at woodworking and with the patience to sand wood and apply many coats of varnish. They take a chassis of nearly any vintage or make and then build a wooden body upon it. In this book, an effort was made to place photos by the year of the chassis. A few of the station wagons shown on older chassis were, in fact, replacements for more conventional auto bodies that had originally been on the chassis. Future collectors will have to determine whether the woody that they are wondering about buying was, in fact, a woody for its entire life.

Ken Gross, director of the Petersen Automotive Museum in Los Angeles: wrote this introduction to the museum's 1999 woody exhibit, and it sums up the timeless appeal of the woody:

It's been decades since Detroit sold real wood-bodied cars, but their fascination lingers like a fond childhood memory. Bobbing in a sea of lozenge-shaped, single hued, boring contemporary metal cars, a gleaming Ford woody wagon, an open-topped Sportsman or a massively proportioned Chrysler Town & Country convertible is a splendid anachronism—a beautifully-finished piece

This 1964 Austin Mini contains a small amount of wood trim. It was seen on the pier at Santa Cruz. Note the miniature surfboard on the roof rack.

of fine furniture on wheels. Russet mahogany panels, honey-toned, abstractly-patterned bird's-eye maple body framing, intricate finger joints, piano-hinged doors, neatly-carved roof pillars, slatted wood headliners, under burnished, tightly tacked boot topping . . . everywhere you look, there's much to admire. Chippendale on wheels? You bet. Passersby stare, smile, and point. And these days, everybody wants one.

If one believes the message in *The Three Little Pigs* tale, one would prefer brick to wood. This circa-1969 VW pickup is covered with a brick pattern and is used to advertise a nearby antiques store in Santa Rosa, California

Wood has been substituted for chrome on this early-1980s Ford pickup. *Tom Brownell*

Wood also has been placed along the sides of the bed. *Tom Brownell*

This circa-1980 Jeep pickup carries a wood-covered camping shell and frame window. Ship-lapping was used to join the exterior skin, which was screwed to an interior frame. The photo was taken near Reno.

This cute wooden body was built on a 1990 Mazda chassis; it was spotted in Kentfield, California.

Note how the taillights of the Mazda fit into the woodwork.

This homemade rig was photographed in 1999 at a car show in Washington State. Its roof is plywood, but the trim appears to be solid wood.

SELECTED BIBLIOGRAPHY

Adamich, Thomas A. "'Woodys,' Workhorses, and the 'Wonderbread' Generation—The Rise and Fall of the Station Wagon and the Emergence of the Minivan." A paper presented at the third biennial Automotive History Conference sponsored by the Society of Automotive Historians, Los Angeles, 2000.

Anheuser-Busch. "Something New Again—The Country Club Body." *ABTatler* (November 1923): page A. This was the employee magazine of Anheuser-Busch.

Briggs, Bruce. *The Station Wagon.* New York: Vantage Press, 1975.

Bunn, Don. *Dodge Trucks.* Osceola, WI: MBI Publishing, 1996.

Burness, Tad. *American Truck & Bus Spotter's Guide 1920-1985.* Osceola, WI: MBI Publishing Company, 1985.

Butler, Don. "Wandering in the Woods." *Cars & Parts* (March 1976): 152–155.

"Cantrell, designer of station wagon, dies," *The Long Islander* (May 16, 1974), section one.

Crismon, Fred W. *International Trucks.* Osceola, WI: MBI Publishing Company, 1995.

Duggan, Edward P. "The Education of American Carriage Makers, 1880–1916." *The Journal of Transport History* (March 1990): 1–11.

Emanuel, Dave. "Station Wagons: The Centaur of Automotive Mythology." *Automobile Quarterly* (first quarter, 1984): 4–43.

Fetherston, David. *American Woodys.* Sebastopol, CA: Thaxton Press Office, 1998.

———. *Woodys.* Osceola, WI: MBI Publishing Company, 1995.

Gross, Ken. "Surf's Up! The Great American Woody." *Petersen* [Automotive Museum] *Quarterly* (summer 1999): 2–5.

"History a Mystery for 1947 *Mil-Col Land Yacht.*" *Old Cars Weekly* (February 15, 1990): 45.

"History of J. T. Cantrell & Company." From the Web site http:dodgepowerwagon.com/woody/cantrell2.html (June 29, 2000). The original apparently appeared in the *Huntington History Review*, November–December 1973.

Kowalke, Ron. *Station Wagon.* Iola, WI: Krause, 1998.

Lamm, Michael. "Wagon Wheels—All American Station Wagons." *Special Interest Autos* (April 2000): 14–23.

Lampert, Toby. "What Makes a Vehicle a Woodie?" *This Old Truck* (May/June 1998): 39

Langworth, Richard M. "Town & Country, Chrysler's Beautiful Land Yacht." *Automobile Quarterly* (third quarter, 1973): 298–309.

"Life and Times of Waterloo's Own Legendary Wooden Body Company." This is based upon recollections of Karl Bernhardt, who had worked for the firm since 1928. The name of the publication where the article appeared and the date are unknown.

Mack, Rick. "Finishing Your Woody: Choices, Procedures and Style." From the Web site http://oldwoodies.com/shoptalk_refinish.htm (September 25, 2000).

Manning, Steve. "A Short History of Station Wagons in the U.S.A." From the Web site http://www.stationwagon.com/history.html (August 28, 2000).

Marmon-Herrington News. Issues from 1944.

Martin-Parry Bodies for Chevrolet. A series of five 10- to 20-page booklets (circa 1927–1930).

Mason, Bill and Mary. "1930 Model A with Distinctive Wildanger Body." *Old Cars Weekly* (January 28, 1988).

Miller, David. "One-ton Mountain Woodie." From the Web site http:www.oldwoodies.com/feature-40gmc.htm (September 25, 2000).

Mroz, Albert. *The Illustrated Encyclopedia of American Trucks and Commercial Vehicles.* Iola, WI: Krause, 1996.

Narus, Donald J. *Great American Woodies & Wagons*. Glen Ellyn, IL: Crestline, 1977.

Northport Historical Society. *Cantrell's `Woodies.'* A flyer produced by the Northport Historical Society. Northport, NY: no date.

Olson, Byron, and Dan Lyons. *Station Wagons*. Osceola, WI: MBI Publishing Company, 2000.

Passenger Bodies on the Speed Wagon Chassis. Lansing, MI: Reo Motor Car Company, 1922.

Rundle, Randy. "Buyer's Guide to Wooden-Body Station Wagons." *Old Cars Weekly* (September 2, 1999): 43.

Sorensen, Lorin, *The Commercial Fords*. St. Helena, CA: Silverado Publishing Company, 1984.

Special Bodies on the Speed Wagon Chassis. Lansing, MI: Reo Motor Car Company, 1922.

Special Equipment for Chevrolet Trucks (The Silver Book) Detroit: Argus Press, 1946.

Special Equipment for Chevrolet Trucks (The Silver Book for 1954) Detroit: Cosgrove and Equipment Associates, 1953.

Speed Wagon Complete with Standard Bodies, The. Lansing: Reo Motor Car Company, 1920.

United Automotive Body Company, Bulletin No. 10. Cleveland: United Automotive Body Company, circa 1920. Describes their suburban body serial number 91.

"Want a Woody? Call George, the Woody Man." *Petersen* [Automotive Museum] *Quarterly* (summer 1999): 6–7.

Robert J. Whittier. "$350 Station Wagon." *Mechanix Illustrated* (October 1950): 130–135, 158.

Edward G. Wildanger. "The Joseph Wildanger Company, Custom Body Builders." Unpublished: no date.

Wood, Donald F. *American Buses*. Osceola, WI: MBI Publishing Company, 1998.

Wren, James A., and Genevieve J. *Motor Trucks of America*. Ann Arbor, MI: University of Michigan Press, 1979.

Yenne, Bill. *Woodies*. Cobb, CA: First Glance Books, 1997.

INDEX

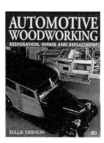

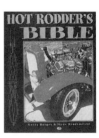